Beds & Borders

40 Professional Designs for Do-It-Yourselfers

Created by
Susan A. Roth & Company

Landscape Designs by
Ireland-Gannon Associates, Inc.

Project Manager:
Damon Scott

Landscape Illustrations by
Ray Skibinski

HOME PLANNERS, LLC
3275 W. INA RD., SUITE 110, TUCSON, ARIZONA 85741

Designed and produced by SUSAN A. ROTH & COMPANY
  3 Lamont Lane
  Stony Brook, NY 11790

  Publisher: Susan A. Roth
  Writers: Jacqueline Murphy and Susan A. Roth
  Designer: Jacqueline Murphy
  Copy Editor: Lynn McGowan

Landscape designs by Ireland-Gannon Associates, Inc.
  Route 25A, Northern Boulevard
  East Norwich, NY 11732

  Designers: Jason Argentieri, Timothy Barry, Jeffrey Diefenbach, Patrick J. Duffe, Frank L. Esposito,
  Janis Leonti, Gary J. Martin, Salvatore Masullo, Jim Morgan, Maria Morrison, Michael J. Opisso,
  Anne Rode, Paul Roedel, Damon Scott

Regional Consultants:
  Northeast: Carol Howe
  Mid-Atlantic: Jacqueline Murphy and Susan A. Roth
  Deep South: Nancy Jacobs Roney
  Midwest: Alan Branhagen
  Florida & Gulf Coast: Robert Haehle
  Rocky Mountains: Allen M. Wilson
  Northern California & Pacific Northwest: Lucy Hardiman
  Southern California & Desert Southwest: Karen Dardick

Artwork:
  Landscape renderings: Ray Skibinski
  Landscape plot plans: Damon Scott

  All photographs by Susan A. Roth

  Cover photo: Landscape design by Kristin Horne

Published by HOME PLANNERS, LLC, wholly owned by Hanley-Wood, LLC
3275 West Ina Road, Suite 110
Tucson, AZ 85741

  President: Jayne Fenton
  Vice President, Group Content: Jennifer Pearce
  Executive Editor: Linda B. Bellamy
  Editorial Director: Arlen Feldwick-Jones
  Managing Editor: Vicki Frank
  Special Projects and Acquisitions Editor: Paulette Dague
  Production Liaison: Jay C. Walsh

10 9 8 7 6 5 4

Printed in the United States of America.

Library of Congress Catalogue Card Number: 97-077458
ISBN softcover 1-881955-45-1

TABLE OF CONTENTS

INTRODUCTION

THE GROUNDS SURROUNDING YOUR HOME are your family's private outdoor living space—a special space that can be designed to be both beautiful and enjoyable. This book will help you bring out your yard's potential to become a lovely retreat, a special place to enjoy outdoor hobbies and gardening activities, or an inviting spot for outdoor entertaining and relaxing, by landscaping small garden areas with beautiful beds and borders. And you'll find out how to take care of your gardens so they require a minimum of maintenance and upkeep.

Beds & Borders is the fourth in a series of unique books. Here, you will find plot plans and illustrations of 40 professionally designed beds and borders for which you can order actual customized blueprints. You can choose to order a full-size, six-page blueprint package for each design complete with a regionalized plant list selected for your area of the country, or use what you learn and see here as an inspiration for creating your own distinctive garden.

This special book is the result of the collaboration of three companies that are well respected in their fields: Home Planners, architects and publishers of blueprints for do-it-yourself home builders and contractors; Susan A. Roth & Company, a horticultural publishing and book packaging company; and Ireland-Gannon Associates, Inc., a nationally recognized, award-winning, landscape design-build firm.

Home Planners, founded in 1946, has published over 150 books of home plans and sold more than 3 million blueprints for their designs. Their home plans are featured regularly in special issues of *House Beautiful, Better Homes and Gardens, Colonial Homes,* and other leading shelter magazines. Their other books of landscape plans are *The*
Home Landscaper, which offers designs for 40 front yards and 15 backyards; *The Backyard Landscaper,* which features 40 backyard designs; and *Easy-Care Landscape Plans,* which features 41 no-fuss designs for front- and backyards.

Susan A. Roth & Company created all these landscape plans for Home Planners and has put together many popular garden books for Ortho Books. The author of *The Weekend Garden Guide—Work-Saving Ways to A Beautiful Backyard* (Rodale Press), *The Four-Season Landscape* (Rodale Press), *The Better Homes & Gardens Complete Guide to Gardening* (Meredith Books), and *The Better Homes & Gardens New Complete Guide to Gardening* (Meredith Books), and a contributor to many publications, Susan A. Roth is also a widely published photographer whose garden photographs appear in many magazines.

Ireland-Gannon Associates, Inc., has been serving the prestigious North Shore of Long Island since 1943. In 1978, the com-pany formed an association with the acclaimed Martin Viette Nursery, a major horticultural center in the Northeast. Ireland-Gannon has been honored with over 80 awards in the last 25 years, including several Grand Awards from the Associated Landscape Contractors of America and Superior Awards from the National Landscape Association.

By using the designs in this book, you'll have no need to hire a landscape architect or designer to create a design for you. Most top-notch firms, such as Ireland-Gannon Associates, Inc., charge between $500 and $1,000 just to design the planting scheme for a half-acre property. For a fraction of that cost, you can order a large professional-quality blueprint package tailored to your needs. Each package comes in eight regionalized versions featuring planting schemes coded with plants that are specially selected to thrive in various parts of the country. (See page 154.)

ABOUT THE DESIGNS IN THIS BOOK

In this book, horticulturists and landscape designers have combined their talents to create 40 professional-quality bed and border designs for the do-it-yourselfer and landscape contractor. The plans offer a range of possibilities for front- and backyards and compact and spacious lots. For your convenience, the plans are divided into several chapters, each with a theme that will help you narrow your choices.

Because many people have difficulty imagining what a one-dimensional planting plan will look like in reality, a full-color illustration accompanies each plot plan. These paintings show the landscape after it has matured and filled in, to give you a sense of the mood and feeling the landscape design will create a few years after installation.

HOW TO USE THIS BOOK

In Chapter 1, you can read about how professionals design beds and borders, so you can better appreciate the features you see in these designs. And if you wish to, you'll learn enough to create your own design from scratch.

In Chapter 2, you'll read about the easiest ways to take care of your beds and borders. If you want to have a beautiful garden but don't have a lot of time to devote to it, you can reduce the time you spend tending it by using these tried-and-true methods. You'll learn the fastest and easiest ways to care for your garden, including the best ways to prune shrubs to slow down their growth rather then speed it up.

Chapters 3 through 10 are the heart of the book and include the plot plans and illustrations of the designs. When you study them, you'll see how the principles dis-

cussed in Chapter 1 are used to create truly useful and attractive beds and borders.

If you would like to install any of these gardens on your own property, you can use the plot plan provided in the book to guide you, modifying it, if necessary, to fit the exact contours of your house and property. It isn't necessary to order the blueprint package offered with each design. However, the six-page package is helpful, since it contains an enlarged, easy-to-use blueprint and a regionalized plant list selected especially for your climate, as well as several pages of information on planting and caring for your new garden.

Chapter 11 tells you how to work with the landscape plans shown here and helps you through the installation process, whether you choose to do the planting and construction yourself or hire a landscape contractor to do the work.

INSTALLING THE PLANS

Most do-it-yourselfers can install any of these bed or border gardens themselves. If you don't want to do the planting or construction yourself, you can hire a landscape contractor—a professional installer—to do the job. Keep in mind that most landscape contractors are not skilled designers, even though they may advertise themselves as such. They are skilled at maintaining a lawn, planting or removing trees, or regrading the land, but when it comes to actual landscape design, their talents may be limited. By using one of the plans in this book— whether you install it yourself or hire a contractor to do it—you can be assured that you are getting a top-quality design, one created by an award-winning landscape design firm. Landscaping is an investment in the enjoyment and value of your home, so why not begin with the best design possible? ❀

Design: Conni Cross

CHAPTER 1

DESIGNING BEDS AND BORDERS

It's always a good idea to start with a design that makes sense, whether it's a design for a house or for a garden. Smart design decisions for a garden differ from those for a house, but the outcome should be the same: you should be happy and comfortable with what you have. And your beds and borders should be designed for minimal maintenance, by matching the plants to your local climate, soil, and exposure. Read on to find out how professionals design successful garden beds and borders that are practical as well as beautiful.

To prevent this island planting from becoming an obstacle in the middle of the lawn, the designer includes a mulched pathway that invites visitors to walk through the bed.

GETTING STARTED

A landscape professional would ask you some important questions before beginning any type of design, but you can go through the process by yourself with the help of this book. Ask yourself these questions, writing down your answers and making lists, if you wish: How much time do you have to tend a garden? What are the growing conditions where you want to install a new bed or border garden? What is your personal style and the style of your house: casual or formal, bold or subdued?

Consider whether or not you want beds or borders to define property boundaries, create privacy, enclose an outdoor dining area, or frame a picturesque scene. Once you know what you want, you can select one of the professionally designed plans in this book or use them as inspiration for designing your own.

DEFINING BEDS AND BORDERS

A bed is a grouping of plants with no vertical elements to delineate it, which means it can be seen from several, or all, sides. A bed must look good from various vantage points. A border differs from a bed in one important regard: a vertical element, such as a wall, a fence, or a hedge, defines one or more sides of a border, creating a back, front, and sides to the garden.

These definitions become important as you look through the book to find the right design or designs for your particular situation. If you'd like to screen a view, a border with a tall evergreen hedge, such as the Colorful Evergreen Border, or a planting on top of a berm, such as the Privacy Berm, would be the best choices. If you're looking for a focal point for your front or backyard, a colorful island bed, such as the Blue-and-Yellow Island Bed, or the Corner Property Planting would be good choices.

ORGANIZING SPACE IN YOUR YARD

Although this book offers designs for beds and borders, as opposed to entire landscapes, it's a good idea to consider your outdoor environment as a whole before plunking down a bed or border wherever there's some spare room.

Landscape designers know that it's best to organize the outdoor spaces in a yard in ways that fulfill many of the same basic needs as the rooms in a house. As with the indoors, the yard should have areas where your family can relax, play, entertain, cook, and dine. You may also want places for storage and pursuing outdoor hobbies, such as vegetable or flower gardening. And, as with the interior decor, the exterior decor is most enjoyable and inviting if it offers an attractive and private environment full of pleasing colors and textures.

A large house can accommodate many different styles and colors without overwhelming the eye, while a smaller home needs a single, cohesive theme to avoid unruly clashes of style and color. The same holds true for a garden. If you have a small yard, stick to one style, whether it's formal or informal. The different parts of your garden should look as though they belong together, one leading to the other, with a sense of order and style appropriate to you and your home. If you have a larger yard, you can install beds and borders with different styles, as long as they are visually separated from each other.

Evaluating the Possibilities

Several factors determine the design of a successful bed or border: available space, existing site and climate, and desired effect or style.

First, determine the location and amount of space you can allocate for a bed or border garden. Carry a tape measure and a pad to jot down measurements and take notes. Take photos from the vantage points from which you will actually view the new garden: from the patio, from the front walkway, from the kitchen window, etc. A photograph can point out things you might not notice on a walking tour of your property.

Once you get the photos developed, spread them out and take a critical look. Does one corner of the yard look bare? Does another area need to have a tree or two removed? You can even draw right on the photos with a grease pencil to experiment with any landscape changes that you're considering.

Next, assess the amount of sunlight and the quality of the soil in the chosen site. If you're removing an existing bed or border to make way for a new design, note the type of plants that thrived in this area, as well as the ones that seemed to struggle. This is an easy way to figure out which kinds of plants to use in your new design.

Observe the path of the sun over the course of the day as it relates to your garden site. Look for shade cast by existing trees, your house, or nearby structures, including fences. You may find that the area gets full sun in the morning while the neighbor's fence casts shade the rest of the day. Remember that the angle of the sun is different in summer than in winter. In winter, days are shorter and the sun is lower in the sky than in summer.

RIGHT DESIGN, RIGHT PLACE

Elements of the landscape should look as if they belong where they are. A cactus garden looks perfectly at home next to an adobe hacienda in an arid landscape; it's low-maintenance as well, because cacti are naturally adapted to thrive in hot, dry environments. A lush, tropical design planted in the same landscape looks out of place, and the amount of water needed to maintain it

Design: Leonna Duff

makes it impractical. Likewise, a neat, formal garden design complements a traditional, symmetrical house nicely, while an exuberant, casual garden might not be as effective.

Color and Style Cues

There are so many plant and design choices to consider, you might feel a bit overwhelmed at first. Start by looking at the existing landscape—both hardscape and softscape—for color and style cues. Color and style in the landscape come not only from the plants but also from your house—whether it's shingled, adobe, or brick—and from other hardscape elements such as walkways, retaining walls, and fences.

First, note the color of your house. The color of the house is especially important when you're designing beds or borders that will function as foundation plantings, or those that are closest to the house, because the walls serve as the backdrop for the plants.

If your house is white and you select all white flowering plants, they'll disappear. Instead, consider planting a border filled with brilliant, jewel-toned flowers for a rich display against the white background,

In the best garden designs, all the elements, including the hardscape materials, match the garden's style. Here, a weathered picket fence and bench contribute to this cottage garden's rustic charm.

Design: Kristin Horne

Artfully using plants with colorful foliage is an easy way to create a garden that remains eye-catching for months. Here, silver and purple foliage plants combine beautifully with blue flowers. Their leaves will be colorful long after the flowers fade.

which is essentially neutral. For a quieter, more serene effect, you could install mainly foliage plants with occasional touches of white flowers to visually link the border to the house.

The style of your house is another useful design cue. A traditional house with a central entry, clearly defined rectilinear lines, and symmetrical windows begs for neat, formal garden beds and borders. A modern house with an asymmetrical entry, curvilinear lines, and varied window patterns calls for informal, more naturalistic garden beds and borders. Many contemporary houses are eclectic in style, which means you, as the designer, have the flexibility to create both informal and formal beds and borders in the surrounding landscape.

Selecting Plants for Beds or Borders

Perhaps the most important elements in a successful design are the plants. It's important to select plants that will suit your site and your aesthetic preferences. Whether you need a tall screen planting that thrives in hot sun or a shrub with pink flowers, be sure to consider the cultural needs of the plants you'd like to install. Plants that are well adapted to the local climate perform best and require the least maintenance.

Use woody plants (trees, shrubs, and vines) to provide the foundation of a bed or border design, and herbaceous plants (perennials, annuals, and bulbs) to provide a changing display of color. Many woody plants also provide color from autumn foliage, berries, variegated foliage, and showy flowers.

When you combine woody and herbaceous plants in the same bed or border,

you'll always have something pretty to look at. But note how the designs in this book combine the perennials with the shrubs: perennials are grouped in the open bays created by widely spaced groups of shrubs, not sprinkled among individual shrubs. This gives the garden a good structure and allows the perennials and shrubs to grow to their full size without crowding each other.

Using Color and Texture for Foliar Impact

Leaves provide texture and color, and can be used to create spatial illusions in a garden. "Texture" refers to the size and character of a plant's leaves, as well as its general form and visual weight. Plants with large, dull leaves and dense branches have more substance than plants with small, shiny leaves and loose branches.

Place fine-textured plants, such as ferns, boxwood, or coreopsis, in a small bed or border in a confined area to create an illusion of spaciousness. Use coarse-textured plants, such as rhododendrons or large-leaved hostas, to make a large bed or border garden in an open area seem closer to the viewer or more intimate. Or use plants with narrow, upright leaves, such as yucca or iris, to add height to a mixed planting.

Plants with colorful foliage can brighten up a garden design or help make smooth transitions between competing colors. Single-color foliage plants, especially those with gray-green leaves, such as many hostas, or silver leaves, such as artemisia, soften the effect of bold flower combinations. Purple-leaved plants, such as 'Crimson Pygmy' barberry and 'Bronze Beauty' bugleweed, make an effective contrast with gold-leaved plants, such as golden English yew or 'Goldmound' spirea.

Plants with multi-colored leaves, such as many hosta cultivars, canna, and caladium, can be just as colorful as flowers and are grown primarily for their foliage. Variegated foliage plants look best when used sparingly and with plenty of solid green to act as a foil.

MIXED BORDERS FOR YEAR-ROUND INTEREST

The best way to create a bed or border that provides year-round interest is to mix a variety of different types of plants in the same garden. That way, you can have a gorgeous late-winter display of bulbs and flowering trees, such as snowdrops and witch hazel, followed by the early-spring growth of emerging perennials, such as hostas, and groundcovers, such as epimedium. Soon, the summer-flowering perennials, such as coreopsis, daylilies, and bellflowers, will be in bloom, followed by the autumnal colors of deciduous shrubs, such as burning bush, and trees, such as maples. Winter changes the focus to more delicate aspects of plant structure, bark, and berries. All this excitement can happen in a single bed or border if you interplant.

You'll need to consider more than just flower color, especially in a mixed border that contains deciduous and berried trees and shrubs. Foliage and fruit color changes over the course of the year and adds other elements to your living palette. Remember that just when many perennials finish flowering in autumn, deciduous trees and shrubs start their fall foliage show. You might have some crossover of perennial flower color with fall foliage color, or spring bulbs with flowering shrubs, so be sure to select colors that work together if they overlap in your bed or border.

Selecting and Using Herbaceous Plants and Bulbs

Annuals, perennials, bulbs, and many groundcovers grow quickly, and their flowers add beauty to the landscape.

Annuals live for one growing season and then die, although some reseed themselves. The charm of annuals is that they'll bloom right up until the first frost, as long as you

The best borders include shrubs and small trees to create height and year-round interest, with flowering perennials and annuals planted in front of and between these taller plants.

Design: Conni Cross

regularly remove spent flowers. Use annuals to provide long-lasting floral color, to fill in blank spots in the garden, or to provide cover for the fading bulb leaves.

Perennials, bulbs, and groundcovers come back every year after going dormant during winter. They generally have a much shorter flowering period than annuals, but offer years of dependable performance. Perennials and bulbs are most effective planted in large drifts of a single color.

As long as their heights and cultural requirements are well matched, you can plant evergreen groundcovers with bulbs and perennials. (For example, tulips that reach 10 to 14 inches tall look great growing through a groundcover that reaches 4 to 8 inches tall.) Then, when the bulbs and perennials are finished flowering or go dormant, the groundcover keeps the garden beautifully neat.

Selecting and Using Ornamental Shrubs

Ornamental shrubs are among the most versatile plants you can use in a mixed bed or border garden. They offer a sense of permanence and stability that sets the tone for the rest of the garden. You can use shrubs to mark boundaries and direct the flow of traffic around a bed or to provide a living backdrop for a border garden, or you can plant them in groups within the main part of the bed or border. You can even plant a bed or border garden that is composed mainly of shrubs, such as the Colorful Evergreen Border (L313) or the Shade-Loving Shrub Garden (L325).

Some evergreen shrubs, such as hollies, provide brightly colored fruit, while others, such as rhododendrons, offer flowers in addition to year-round greenery. Deciduous flowering shrubs offer flower color, usually in spring or early summer, and many provide bright fall foliage color or berries. When they are leafless in winter, deciduous shrubs have less visual weight than they do in summer.

The designers of the beds and borders in this book use shrubs whose mature size is in scale with the garden, and you should, too. Check with your local nursery or consult a garden reference book to find out the mature sizes of any shrubs you're considering. You'll save time and avoid the need for constant pruning if you select the right-sized shrub for the location you have in mind.

Selecting and Using Ornamental Trees

Ornamental flowering trees, such as magnolias, dogwoods, and crabapples, are usually showier and smaller than shade or street trees. They provide floral color mostly in late winter or spring, followed by bird-attracting fruits and bright foliage in autumn. As with shrubs, orna-

Besides contributing flowers, fruits, and foliage to a garden's design, deciduous shrubs, such as lace-cap hydrangea, create year-round structure with their trunks and branches.

Design: Conni Cross

mental flowering trees give structure to a bed or border garden. Placed centrally as a single specimen in a bed or border, an ornamental tree can establish a formal tone. When planted in naturalistic groves, a grouping of small trees sets a more casual tone.

Because an ornamental tree in a mixed bed or border garden is almost always the tallest element, the tree serves as a focal point. Designers often use ornamental trees to draw attention to a particular part of the garden or to help provide privacy.

Tree trunks add a vertical element to a mixed bed or border, while branches keep your eye from drifting entirely skyward. Weeping tree forms, in particular, draw your eye downward and help focus attention on shorter herbaceous plants.

Select trees whose mature height and spread suit your intended design. If you're placing a tree—even a small one—in a mixed bed or border garden, consider the shade it will eventually cast. Keep this factor in mind when selecting the perennials, annuals, and bulbs you'll want to plant underneath, or near, the tree.

LAYERING BY HEIGHT

The easiest way to show off plants in a bed or border garden is to plant them according to height, with the taller, more massive plants in the background, mid-height plants in the mid-ground, and shortest plants in the foreground. If you have an island bed or any garden that is visible from more than one side, install the tallest plants in the center, with shorter plants around the outside.

In the Background

Larger shrubs—whether evergreen, such as yews, or deciduous, such as lilacs—placed at the back of a border furnish a good background for shorter plants and provide a visual anchor. Taller perennials, such as

hollyhocks or meadow rue, or even towering annuals, such as cleome or sunflowers, make effective background plantings, too. Place background plantings in a neat row with drifts of perennials and annuals in front for a formal effect. Or install background plants in irregular groups for a more casual look.

In the Middle

Plant showy shrubs, perennials, annuals, and bulbs of middle height in drifts, in front of and between the taller background plantings. Some good choices include smaller shrub roses and dwarf azaleas; daylilies and hostas; nicotiana and marigolds; and daffodils and tulips. Placing these mid-height plants along the spine of a garden won't obscure the taller plants in the background, and you'll be able to appreciate their wonderful flowers and foliage at closer range.

When designing a bed or border, arrange the plants in layers, by height. Use a small tree as a tall vertical element, then arrange shrubs beneath its branches, and perennials and groundcovers in front of and between the shrubs.

Design: Tom Pellett

In the Foreground

Whether you choose to edge your bed or border with a permanent structural element, such as brick or stone, or simply cut a clean edge with an edging tool, select plants that will enhance the edge of the garden. (See page 20 for edging techniques.) The lowest plants belong in the foreground, softening the skirts of midground plants.

Edging or foreground plants can spill out onto a walkway for an informal effect, or be neatly trimmed for a formal effect. Traditional choices include a low hedge of neatly clipped dwarf boxwood, germander, or lavender. Lamb's ears, cheddar pinks, the smaller hostas, or one of the many short ornamental grasses, such as blue fescue, also make neat edgings without the need for shearing. Some low-growing annuals, such as curly parsley, sweet alyssum, and edging lobelia, tend to flow nicely and are good for softening the edge of a garden.

To keep paths from spilling over into garden beds, hold the path material in place with an edging. Here, a bender-board edging keeps the wood-chip path neat.

Drawing the Line

Formal beds and borders are generally geometrically perfect shapes, such as rectangles and circles. Use stakes and string to create formal beds with perfectly aligned edges. Informal beds and borders depend on naturalistic, usually curving—sometimes serpentine—lines to create a casual effect. Use garden hoses laid on the ground to create natural-looking curves. Or draw the lines of your new garden by walking along with an open container of garden lime and allowing it to dribble out as you walk.

As you lay out the lines of your bed or border, consider the width and depth. A garden should be visually pleasing and easily accessible for performing routine maintenance chores, such as weeding and deadheading. Professionals recommend adding a narrow maintenance path (1 to 2 feet wide is sufficient) or a series of stepping-stones in gardens that are wider than 4 or 5 feet. Another rule of thumb for size is to make the depth of your garden at least twice the height of the tallest plant you plan to install. For example, if the tallest plant is 6 feet, make the bed or border 12 feet deep.

Establishing a Sense of Rhythm

A sense of visual rhythm in a bed or border invites your eye to move along the length and width of the garden in a leisurely, yet orderly, manner and encourages you to view the entire design as a whole. Landscape designers establish a sense of visual rhythm or movement by alternating strong design elements with more delicate ones, and by repeating colors and drifts, or massed groupings, of plants.

For example, you can plant several drifts of tall pink tulips and sweet woodruff at roughly equal distances from each other along the length and width of a border. This kind of repetition of color and texture provides a sense of organization that is visually pleasing. To create effective drifts, group odd numbers of at least three plants together. Smaller perennials and bulbs look better in drifts of five or nine. The idea is to avoid a polka-dot effect by using generous amounts of plants in each drift.

CREATING BALANCE

A balanced design has a sense of visual stability. Landscape designers achieve balance by siting elements according to their color, texture, and size, as well as their visual mass or weight. Creating a formal, symmetrical design is one way to achieve balance. Or you might prefer an asymmetrical design that is also balanced but more informal. For example, a long, curving border may have a small gazebo at one end. The other end of the border could be balanced by an ornamental tree or grouping of shrubs that is visually equal in mass to the gazebo.

CREATING FOCAL POINTS

Nothing in a landscape catches the eye and imagination as much as a partly obscured garden bench or gazebo mysteriously peeking out from behind a curtain of flowering vines. Even garden furnishings—such as benches, stone walls, birdbaths, garden statuary, arbors, trellises, and fountains— that are completely visible tend to draw attention to themselves and are strong focal points. People perceive these elements as destinations and instinctively want to take a closer look.

For maximum impact, site benches, arbors, and other furnishings where they can be seen from a distance, or from inside the house, and so that visitors will be drawn to the surrounding garden. The

same garden furnishings you use to create focal points also function as permanent structural elements, especially during the colder months of the year, when perennials are out of bloom and deciduous trees are leafless.

Larger plants, such as flowering trees and shrubs, tall perennials, and ornamental grasses, also make effective focal points. Place a single specimen plant in a mixed bed or border where it can act as a punctuation mark to the design or to visually anchor the garden. Focal points, whether they are softscape or hardscape elements, are most intriguing when they are placed either centrally in a design or noticeably off center. Objects or plants that are only slightly off center tend to look unbalanced.

WORKING WITH COLOR

Color can elicit strong emotional responses. While there are some useful ground rules for mixing and matching colors, feel free to experiment. Try this fun and easy way to help you decide on color combinations: pick or buy a bunch of flowers and foliage plants in the colors you're considering, then

A garden is most pleasing when it has a sense of structure and form. You can create structure with sight lines that direct the eye toward a sculpture, bench, fountain, or specimen plant. Here, the lawn path and beds direct your eye toward the stone fountain.

arrange them in a vase to see how they work together. You can even bring the arrangement out to the garden area you're working on and see how the colors look *in situ*.

Color Terminology and Temperature

It's useful to know some basic terminology to help you work with color. The three primary colors—blue, red, and yellow—can be combined to create all the other colors in the rainbow. The farther away you get from the three primary colors, the more interesting and delicate hues you'll discover.

Colors are sometimes described in terms of temperature. Cool colors include shades of green, blue, and violet. Warm colors include shades of red, orange, and yellow. Cool, pastel colors appear to recede, while warm, bright colors appear to pop out, making them seem closer than they really are. You can use cool colors to create a feeling of serenity and calm, or warm colors to create an atmosphere that's lively and festive.

Study the color wheel on this page to get a sense of what you're working with. The color wheel represents the natural color spectrum that you see in every rainbow. The spectrum ranges from the darkest indigo blue to the palest yellow, with gently graduated tones in between.

The color wheel represents the colors of the spectrum. When you combine colors that are directly opposite each other on the wheel, the effect is bold and exciting. When you combine colors that are next to each other, the effect is more serene.

Color Schemes

There are several ways to approach the use of color in a garden: monochromatic, dichromatic, polychromatic, analogous, and complementary. You may want to try one color scheme in the front yard and a completely different scheme in the backyard. Remember to take your color cues from the other dominant elements in the existing landscape.

A monochromatic scheme, such as a garden planted entirely with white-flowered plants, focuses on a single color. A monochromatic bed or border is probably the easiest type to create. All you need to do is decide on a color and select plants that fit into your scheme. If you decide to create a white garden, for example, you could select a range of white-flowered and white-variegated plants so you'll have white touches throughout your garden year-round. Use plants with silvery foliage, such as artemisia, or glistening white bark, such as birch, to add a bit of sparkle to a white scheme.

A dichromatic plan uses two colors. Use any two colors you especially like together. Blue and yellow, violet and blue, or pink and white are some of the many lovely color combinations possible. A polychromatic design employs several or many different colors. Most of the designs in this book are polychromatic—that is, they incorporate a wide range of colors in a single bed or border.

An analogous scheme uses colors that are next to each other on the color wheel, such as blue, violet, and red, or red, orange, and yellow. Use this kind of color scheme where you want to achieve a subtle, almost watercolor effect. Select many different gradations of each color, from dark to light, so that the colors will appear to blend seamlessly into each other.

A complementary design uses colors that are opposite each other on the color wheel, such as orange and blue, or yellow and purple. You'll see that if you place primary colors side by side, such as blue with red, you'll get rather loud results, because the colors appear to vie with each other for your eye's attention. This is the kind of visual conflict that can be quite striking and effective if used sparingly, because your eye is immediately drawn to it. For a more serene effect with two colors, try a dichromatic scheme with two closely related colors, such as blue and violet.

USING AND ADAPTING DESIGNS

This book can help you beautify your yard by providing information on designing and installing garden beds or borders for various locations on your property. If you find a design you'd like to install, you may order large, detailed blueprints with a regionalized plant list for any of the 40 beds and borders featured in this book. (See page 154 for ordering information.)

The garden designs are organized into eight chapters that focus on different land-scaping situations and design objectives, ranging from considerations of privacy to low-maintenance or shady areas. Before you begin preparing new beds or digging up the present ones, consider your existing conditions and your goals. Once you know what you already have and what you'd like to create, you'll be able to choose the design or designs that suit you best.

If you have a large space to fill, you have the fortunate opportunity to plant several beds or borders. Even if you have limited space, it's possible to adapt the designs in this book to fit. See Chapter 11 for information about adapting a design to your particular site. ❁

This spring garden paints itself in a pleasing yellow-and-violet color scheme, based on colors that are opposite each other on the color wheel.

Design: Susan Beard

CHAPTER 2

MAINTENANCE
TECHNIQUES AND TIPS

*There's no such thing as a
maintenance-free garden. But you can
design a garden that requires minimal or
low maintenance and that looks
just as lovely as one needing more care.
All the bed and border designs in this book
are intended to maximize the pleasurable
parts of gardening and minimize
the really hard chores. Once you start
using the various time- and work-saving
techniques in this chapter, you'll discover
that yard maintenance can be a manageable
and enjoyable part of home ownership.
Best of all, efficient maintenance
leaves you with plenty of leisure time
to enjoy your beautiful landscape.*

*A shrub border offers loads of springtime flowers and fall foliage—
and it's easier to maintain than a perennial border, especially if a
heavy mulch is used to keep weeds out and soil moisture in.*

strip of sod. This leaves a handsome, beveled edge around your beds that will keep invasive grass roots away, and you can compost the sod you remove.

Or you might prefer to install an edging strip of vinyl, steel, or wood, or a mowing strip of brick. The best edging strips do their job of keeping garden edges neat as inconspicuously as possible. Garden supply stores offer a wide variety of easy-to-install and unobtrusive edging strips.

A brick mowing strip that the lawn mower's wheels can ride upon shows off a garden by creating a formal edge. It also makes mowing easier by eliminating the need to hand trim the lawn's edges.

NEAT BEDS AND BORDERS

Mixed beds and borders contain different types of plants that need different kinds of attention. The following information will help you keep your new bed or border looking great year after year. Review the chart on page 25 to help you plan your garden activities.

Clean Edges

Edging a flower bed or border is a handsome and practical way of keeping grass roots from invading it and becoming a weed problem. Edging also keeps vigorous perennials and groundcovers from spilling over into your lawn. You can create a clean edge by using a tool, such as a half-moon edger or sharp-edged spade, or by installing a permanent physical element, such as an edging strip or a mowing strip.

To make a clean edge by hand, take a sharp-edged spade or a half-moon edger with a sharp blade, and press it straight down into the soil, 2 or 3 inches deep. Then push down on the handle, and pry up a

Whatever type of edging strip you choose, make sure you install the strip flush with the soil level or only slightly above it. That way, you'll be able to mow right out to the edge of the lawn and avoid the chore of hand-trimming the lawn edges.

Vinyl edging strips in neutral colors, such as dark green, brown, or black, with a rounded top edge, are a good choice, since they will blend well with the lawn.

Steel edging is the most durable, as well as the most expensive, but the initial investment will pay off in the long run. Steel edging may look a bit stark when first installed, but it eventually weathers to a natural-looking reddish brown.

A third alternative for edging material is wood. For example, railroad ties or landscape timbers can be sunk into the ground and make wonderful edging and mowing strips. Unlike vinyl and steel, however, this type of wood is rigid and therefore useful only for straight-sided beds and borders.

To install vinyl or steel edging or railroad ties, dig a trough deep enough so that the edging is flush with the soil level. Lay the edging into the trough and backfill with soil. Firm the soil into place with your feet.

Bender board, as the name implies, is bendable and can be used to form the edges of curved beds and borders. It's available at lumber yards and is best used in layers of at least three boards.

To install bender board, dig a trough as you would for vinyl or steel edging strips. Place the layers of boards into the trough. Then pound stakes into the soil on either side of the boards at 3-foot intervals.

A properly installed mowing strip accomplishes two goals: it keeps grass from sneaking into flower beds and borders, and it provides a flat surface for lawn mower wheels to travel.

Here's how to install bricks to create a practical, attractive mowing strip:

- Use paving bricks, which hold up against the rigors of weather and direct contact with the soil.

- Dig a trench deep enough to accommodate a double row of staggered bricks with an inch or two of sand covering the bottom of the trench. (You might want to add a layer of landscape fabric over the sand to discourage weeds.)

- Lay the first row of bricks very close together, lengthwise on their edges.

- Lay the next row of bricks perpendicular to the first row, on their faces, or the broad side of each brick.

THE BENEFITS OF MULCHING

Mulching is probably the easiest of all garden chores, and possibly the best thing you can do for your garden. Mulch is a layer of organic or inorganic material placed on the soil beneath plants. Mulch smothers weeds, thus reducing the need for weeding. It also helps keep the soil moist, by reducing evaporation, which saves on watering.

A 2- to 4-inch layer of loose material insulates the soil, protecting surface roots from heat in summer, and from frost damage and heaving (being lifted from the ground by freezing and thawing soil) in winter. Mulch also protects plants from diseases, by keeping soil-borne pathogens from splashing onto the leaves.

Organic Mulches

Organic mulches, such as compost, wood chips, shredded leaves, and aged manure, slowly release valuable nutrients into the soil, reducing the need for fertilizing. Compost also adds beneficial, disease-fighting organisms to the soil.

When using fresh organic mulches, add nitrogen-rich fertilizers to the area to replenish the nutrients these mulches use as they decompose. Because organic mulches break down, you'll need to refresh the mulch every year or so. Add a layer of new mulch in spring or early summer to maintain a depth of 2 to 4 inches.

A mulch of fine-textured wood chips dresses up a garden bed while serving several practical purposes: it prevents dirt from splashing on the blossoms, smothers weeds, and keeps the soil moist and cool.

Inorganic Mulches

Inorganic mulches include crushed rock or gravel, and synthetic landscape fabrics. These mulches suppress weeds, but offer little insulation and no nutrients for plant roots, and can actually cook some plants. Crushed rock and gravel look best when used to cover paths or large, unplanted areas, or placed around plants in rock gardens and arid landscapes.

Landscape fabrics are not meant to be used alone; put them under loose mulches for added weed suppression. Use landscape fabric under trees and shrubs only where you intend the covering to be permanent. Surface roots can be damaged when the fabric is removed because they sometimes weave themselves into the fabric.

In sites where the soil is loamy and the beds well mulched, rainfall is often sufficient to meet the garden's needs. To supplement rain in other sites, an in-ground sprinkler or drip-irrigation system saves time.

WATERING WISDOM

Few climates can provide consistent moisture on a weekly basis. And while most plants can go for a few days without water, many begin to go dormant, lose roots, and even die if drought lasts for a few weeks or more. Gardeners must step in and irrigate landscape plants when necessary.

It's better to water infrequently but deeply—say, one good soaking a week—than to apply small amounts of water every few days. Apply enough water to penetrate the soil about 18 inches. Wetting only the soil surface weakens plants by encouraging shallow, drought-vulnerable roots to form.

You can reduce the number of waterings by working organic matter, such as compost or leaf mold, into the soil to improve your soil's moisture retention. Adding organic matter is especially beneficial in the case of sandy soils, which have a low organic content and do not retain water.

Deciding When to Water

To determine if a plant needs water, the time-tested method is to stick your finger into the soil within the plant's root zone. In the case of most annuals and shallow-rooted perennials, it's probably time to water if the soil feels dry an inch below the soil surface. This method works, but if your garden is sizable, use a stick instead of your finger.

Here's a neat trick for telling at a glance if it's time to water: For each group of plants in your garden, include one or more "indicator" plants, such as phlox, that you know wilt quickly when the soil dries out. As you make the rounds in your garden, observe the indicator plants, and give them—and the plants growing nearby—a drink as soon as they start to droop.

PREVENTING WEEDS

Bare soil is at the mercy of drying sunlight and erosion caused by wind and rain, so nature protects the soil by covering it with plants. We call these unwanted plants "weeds." So expect to find weeds growing in any garden site that you leave bare. You can fight weeds effectively by:

- Covering garden soil with weed-smothering mulch.

- Planting a dense group of low-growing groundcovers beneath trees and shrubs, and even under perennials and bulbs.

- Laying down plastic sheeting, landscape fabric, or several sheets of newspaper beneath a gravel or mulch path.

If a few weeds poke up through the mulch or groundcover, they will be easy to hand-pull when the soil is moist from rain or watering. If stubborn perennial weeds keep coming back from underground runners, try pouring boiling water on their roots.

Weeds can be killed with the systemic herbicide glyphosate, which is sold under various trade names. This herbicide remains in the plant's tissues and does not move through the soil. It also quickly breaks down, so is relatively safe to use.

When using glyphosate or any herbicide, follow label directions carefully. Use only on windless days, and take care not to splash it on desirable plants, because most herbicides kill plants indiscriminately.

Managing Pests and Diseases

The plants selected for the designs in this book are as disease- and insect-resistant as they are easy to care for. When you start with resistant plants, half the battle is won. Keeping plants healthy is also important, since pests and diseases will seek out weaker victims. By simply providing plants with the type of soil, drainage, nutrients, and moisture they require, you'll help strengthen them so they can survive an occasional attack.

Many of the routine maintenance-saving techniques described in this chapter also protect against pests and diseases. For example, mulching, which keeps soil-borne

To reduce weeding chores, grow a thick groundcover between stepping stones and beneath shrubs and trees.

pathogens from splashing onto plants, and watering deeply, which encourages healthy root development, both help to make plants strong enough to resist pest and disease attacks.

Try washing garden plants off regularly with a vigorous spray of water from the hose, making sure you hit both upper and lower sides of leaves. This actually knocks off tiny, sap-sucking insects and disease spores. Be sure to spray plants in the morning so that they have time to dry by sundown; many diseases thrive on foliage that stays wet overnight, when the air is cool.

It's also helpful to keep your garden clean. By removing dead leaves and other plant debris, not only are you keeping the garden tidy, you are also eliminating a favorite breeding ground for all sorts of pests and diseases—and you'll have the makings for great compost.

Even well-maintained gardens with healthy plants have occasional problems. When you encounter pests or diseases, the easiest option is to tolerate light damage. If a few leaves are spotted with fuzzy, white, or sooty, black fungal spots, simply pick and destroy them to keep the problem from spreading. Pick off large leaf-chewing pests

Prune spring-flowering shrubs, such as lilacs, immediately after they bloom; pruning later in the year means you risk removing the following year's flower buds.

with gloved hands and drop them into a jar of soapy water.

If the damage threatens your plants' health, identify the culprits and take appropriate action. You'll find good basic information in the pest and disease guides sold at garden centers. Or, if you prefer, you can snip off an affected leaf and take it to your local Cooperative Extension Agent to have the critters identified and receive recommendations for treatment.

PLANT CARE

Once you've installed your new garden bed or border, you'll need to know how to care for the plants it contains. Generally, you'll have to pay a bit more attention to herbaceous plants than woody plants, since the former require deadheading and fertilizing. However, you'll also need to prune woody plants to keep them looking their best for many years. Some general plant care guidelines follow. For care of specific or more exotic plants, consult your local nursery or a good reference book.

CARING FOR TREES AND SHRUBS

Once established, trees and shrubs require minimal attention to thrive. Generally, all you'll need to do is prune them from time to time to maintain their shape and their health. Trees and shrubs usually don't require nutrients beyond what the soil supplies. However, they'll benefit from any organic mulch you add to your mixed bed or border, as well as any fertilizer you apply to the surrounding annuals and perennials.

Winter is the best time to prune most trees and shrubs. In late winter, your landscape may look like it's still asleep, but it's on the verge of bursting into buds, flowers, and leaves. It's much easier to prune deciduous trees and shrubs before this new growth begins, since you can see where you're cutting more clearly. Also, if you wait too long, the rising sap "bleeds" from the pruning cuts and can invite diseases and pests.

You can prune summer-flowering shrubs and trees in late winter or early spring without sacrificing flowers, because the flower buds form during the present growing season. Wait to prune spring bloomers, such as forsythias, quinces, and lilacs, until after they bloom so you won't lose the flowers, which develop from overwintering buds. Don't wait too long, though; if you prune in late summer or fall, you may cut off next year's flower buds.

Correct Pruning

Pruning is not a task to be undertaken lightly, though it is not all that difficult. Once you understand the basics, pruning is a very satisfying garden activity.

There are basically two types of pruning: thinning and shearing. Thinning cuts do just that: when you thin a plant, you selectively remove branchlets or entire branches, usually with hand or pruning shears, to allow light and air to enter the center of the plant. Use

Season	Equipment, Advice, and Benefits
Late Winter	
Prune shrubs	Hand shears, loppers, or pruning saw; you'll get a clear view for removing dead and damaged branches; prune woody plants that bloom in summer
Cut back grasses, perennials	Hedge shears or string trimmer; makes fast work of cutting dead plants back to a couple of inches above ground before they send up new growth
Order seeds and plants	Mail-order garden catalogs; you'll get more plants, earlier flowers, interesting cultivars for less money than nursery plants; follow packet instructions
Early Spring	
Fertilize bulbs with N-P-K	Commercial or organic fertilizer; early application of fertilizer fuels fast growth and feeds bulbs for next year's flowers
Late Spring	
Prune, deadhead	Hand shears, loppers, or pruning saw; thin spring-flowering shrubs after flowers fade; deadhead most bulbs, allowing only species bulbs to set seed
Divide perennials	Spade or garden fork; multiply plants without buying new ones; divide overgrown clumps to increase flowering and maintain health
Prepare new beds	Garden fork, shovel, garden rake; compost; apply amendments with a shovel; turn soil with a fork; break up clods and level soil with a garden rake
Fertilize perennials, annuals	Balanced, slow-release fertilizer granules or time-release pellets; saves time, ensures healthy plants with plentiful flowers
Early Summer	
Set out plants after last frost	Trowel; annuals started indoors from seed; nursery plants; wait until soil warms to prevent plants from sulking
Apply mulch	Compost, leaf mold, gravel, bark chips, pine needles, grass clippings; mulch suppresses weeds, keeps soil moist and cool
Summer	
Support plants	Use stakes or combine plants for support; plant floppy plants and vines next to sturdy plants; providing natural support saves work
Control weeds	Use hoe or hand cultivator, hand-pull, or smother with barrier
Deadhead	Light-weight pruning shears; remove spent flowers to encourage rebloom
Irrigate during dry periods	"Leaky" hoses, sprinklers, timer; using watering devices attached to timers saves effort by watering on schedule
Battle bugs and diseases	Identify problems in a book, or take sample to Cooperative Extension Office; good garden hygiene and a watchful eye save money and plant health
Edge beds and borders	Edging tool; sharp spade; slice through sod to remove grass roots from bed edges; keeps grass from invading beds and borders
Early Autumn	
Plant bulbs	Spade or narrow-bladed trowel; dig holes and place several bulbs side by side for natural-looking drifts
Fertilize bulbs	Bulb booster fertilizer; encourages healthy root formation
Late Autumn	
Overwinter tender plants	Hand shears, pots, potting medium, trowel; take cuttings or dig up treasured plants to grow indoors over winter; saves money on replacements
Clean up garden	Hand pruners, leaf rake; remove and compost plant debris; protects plant health by removing overwintering sites for pests and diseases
Early Winter	
Mulch	Apply fresh mulch once soil is frozen; prevents soil from heaving

Thinning an evergreen shrub with one-handed clippers, by removing lengths of stems from where they branch in the shrub's interior, controls size without stimulating excessive growth.

The resulting growth is natural-looking and dense, with leaves deep in the shrub's center. Thinned shrubs grow slowly and need pruning only once every year or two.

thinning cuts when you want to maintain the plant's natural shape and for plants with large leaves, such as rhododendrons.

Shearing cuts are more indiscriminate: you just trim off the areas of the plant that you want to remove. This sort of pruning is used to maintain the shape of small-leaved hedge plants, such as boxwood. Use hedge shears—electric-, gas-, or hand-powered—to make quick work of shearing.

You can reduce the need to prune by choosing plants that are the right size and shape for their sites. That means selecting naturally compact, shapely shrubs, or slow-growing, dwarf, or narrow and upright-growing. Then all you need to do is occasionally remove dead or damaged branches, and thin lightly every few years to remove unproductive stems.

If you are new to shrub pruning, go at it slowly at first. As you are pruning, step back and review your work to avoid making drastic mistakes.

How to Thin

Thinning saves time in the long run, because you don't have to repeat the process as often as you would if you sheared the shrubs. Properly thinning a plant allows it to grow at its own pace, and keeps its natural shape, making less work for you. Thinned shrubs also look better than those that are sheared into unnatural shapes, because they have more interior leaves and a fluffier appearance.

To thin a deciduous shrub, first cut to the ground any damaged, dead, non-productive branches. Shrubs that grow by sending up a thicket of stems need to be pruned every few years by cutting a third of the oldest or weakest canes where they emerge from the ground: this reinvigorates the shrub without really controlling its size. To reduce size, cut long branches back to their points of origin on the main trunk, or to where they form a Y with another branch. To totally renew a deciduous shrub, cut it completely to the ground in early spring, leaving 6-inch-tall trunks.

Broadleaf evergreen shrubs, such as rhododendrons, camellias, mountain pieris, and hollies, can also be thinned by cutting stems back to the branch angles. To renew an older shrub, cut one-third of the stems to the ground each year for three consecutive years.

Pruning evergreen shrubs with hedge shears results in flat-sided, formal-looking plants. Shearing stimulates rapid growth only near the cut ends of the stems, while the shrubs' centers are usually devoid of leaves. The rapid growth means you must shear repeatedly every year to keep the plants looking neat.

How to Shear

To shear a formal hedge, you need a good eye, a steady hand, and a tool you're comfortable using. Whether you choose gas-, electric-, or hand-powered hedge shears, make sure the blades are clean and sharp.

Prune formal hedges to create a flat, rounded, or pointed top, with sides that flare slightly toward the bottom to allow light and air to reach the lower branches. If you live in a cold-winter climate, consider shearing hedges with rounded or pointed tops, because they shed snow better than flat tops. You'll need to shear formal hedges at least once a year to keep them neat, more often for faster-growing plants.

Some woody plants, such as boxwood, will not resprout from old wood, so shear back to wood that is still green in the center. Other woody plants, such as yew and privet, will resprout after they are sheared back severely to old wood.

CARING FOR PERENNIALS

Over the course of their life spans, perennials will need to be fertilized, divided, deadheaded, and possibly staked or supported. Read on for information about what tasks you'll need to do, how to do them, and when to perform them so that your perennials will always look their best.

Fertilizing Perennials

Fertilizers have varying proportions of the three major elements that plants need for healthy growth: nitrogen, phosphorus, and potassium (abbreviated as N-P-K). The proportion of N-P-K is noted on the label as a series of numbers, such as 5-10-5, which is a good formula to use for perennials.

In order for perennials to grow well, survive tough winters, and flower year after year, they need a steady supply of nutrients. If you feed them just what they need and no more, you'll spend less money and more time enjoying a healthier, more beautiful garden.

Although slow-release fertilizers are more expensive than soluble commercial fertilizers (which have similar formulations), they are a real time-saver: they don't have to be applied nearly as often and can be used to supplement organic mulches. Like organic soil amendments, slow-release fertilizers break down slowly, gradually releasing their nutrients to plants. Be sure to stop all fertilizing in late summer to let plants "harden off," that is, prepare for their winter dormancy.

Apply a balanced slow-release fertilizer in late spring. Simply scatter the pellets on the surface of the soil and scratch it in lightly. Rain and irrigation water will slowly leach nutrients from the pellets into the soil. Your perennials won't need more until they bloom later in the summer—and this one application will be enough for the foliage plants.

There are several brands of balanced, pelletized, time-released fertilizers available at garden centers. Although they are more expensive than traditional fertilizers, they can last for three months or more.

Supporting Perennials

Weak-stemmed plants or those in windy sites may need to be staked as the season progresses. Anticipate the problem in spring by sticking "pea branches," wooden or metal stakes, or metal grids into the soil where floppy perennials, such as peonies, are emerging. (Pea branches are twiggy dead tree or shrub branches saved from late-winter prunings.) If you install the support early in the growing season, the leaves of the plant will grow up and around to camouflage the device.

Another easy way to provide support is to plant vines or floppy plants, like clematis vines or balloon flowers, with stiff plants, like shrub roses. By allowing the vines or floppy plants to wind through or lean on the stiff plants, you can save yourself the work of staking and enjoy the handsome combinations of flower colors, too.

Dividing Perennials

If you've done everything you can to keep your bulbs and perennials happy and healthy, they will multiply. New plants will form around the original clumps of these plants. Typically, after three to five years, the clumps become crowded, the centers begin to die out, and flower production decreases. When this happens, you'll need to dig the clumps up in spring or fall and divide them into individual plants. Discard the spent, old plants at the center and replant the new ones.

Rejuvenating Perennials

As your flowers begin to fade, keep the plants looking tidy and encourage more flowers by deadheading, or removing old blossoms. Use pruning shears or scissors to remove individual faded flowers near the main stem. You can remove tall, leafless flower stems, such as those of iris, at the base.

To stimulate a new flush of blossoms on perennials with many flowers, such as coreopsis, use hedge shears to shear plants back by about one-quarter to one-third of their size.

When perennials start to look tired or ratty after flowering, you can cut them back

Divide perennials, such as hostas, in spring when new shoots emerge. Dig up the root system and pull or cut it into sections, each containing one or more growing points, or crowns. Replant each section, spacing them to allow plenty of growing room.

hard; as long as you see new growth near the base of the plant. Cut these perennials back to a couple of inches tall after they bloom, and they will send up a neat mound of fresh, new foliage.

CARING FOR BULBS

While you wait for most of your plants to awaken in early spring, spring-flowering bulbs are in their glory. You may not think your bulbs need any attention so soon, but if you apply nitrogen-rich fertilizer when the new foliage pokes through the ground, it fuels their foliage growth, and helps them store food for strong blooming performance next spring.

In fall, apply bulb booster fertilizer, a balanced slow-release plant food, to help the bulbs grow a good root system. Do not use the traditional bone meal, which is not balanced and attracts animal pests.

As the bulb flowers begin to fade, snip off the drooping flowers. But when the leaves begin to turn yellow in late spring or early summer, resist the impulse to remove them. Wait until the bulb leaves turn completely yellow before gently pulling them from the ground. (Don't tie or braid daffodil leaves, because that shields them from the light they need to grow well.)

Better yet, try this low-maintenance trick: interplant bulbs with fast-growing, leafy perennials, like daylilies or hostas. The handsome leaves of these plants shoot up and hide the drooping bulb leaves as they yellow and become unsightly.

PUTTING BORDERS TO BED

Fall, like spring, is a busy time in the garden. Dusting your spring-flowering bulbs with fertilizer again in autumn will give them an energy boost when they wake up in the spring. And, of course, you'll want to

Remove flowers from large-flowered bulbs, such as tulips and daffodils, when they begin to fade. This deadheading prevents seed formation and channels the plant's energy into developing strong bulbs and more flowers the following year.

plant new bulbs now, too.

If you have precious tender plants that you'd like to save for next summer, now's the time to dig them up and put them in pots to bring indoors to overwinter on a sunny windowsill.

If you are growing herbs, vegetables, or late-flowering annuals and want to keep them going as long as possible, cover them with old bedsheets or synthetic floating row covers in the evening when frost threatens. Pull the coverings off in the morning.

Autumn is also the time to protect plants from frost damage. Applying a 4-inch-thick layer of fresh mulch after the ground freezes will help keep plants from being heaved from the soil. If you have shrubs that are exposed to drying winds, you can protect them by wrapping them in burlap or spraying the leaves or needles with an antidessicant, available at garden centers. To make sure the plants are dormant when treating them, wait to apply this product until temperatures fall below freezing.

Late winter is the time to cut back ornamental grasses and any perennials that you left in the garden for winter interest. Using a pair of hand shears, cut back grasses and perennials to an inch or two above the base of the individual plant. If the foliage you've removed is free of insects and disease, you can compost the clippings.

The Right Tool for The Job

No matter what time of year you're doing landscape chores, you'll save time and effort if you have the best quality tools.

Whenever possible, shop for hand tools in a store, rather than by mail. That way, you can try them on, much as you would try on a pair of shoes. If you're buying a shovel, for example, take one off the rack and see how it fits. If it's too heavy or too tall, chances are you'll never use it. For smaller adults, high-quality children's tools are often a better choice. Good tools last a lifetime—or two—and you can often find high-quality, hand-forged garden tools at bargain prices, if you keep a sharp eye out at thrift shops and yard sales.

There's an incredible number of specialized tools available for every possible gardening chore, but you really don't need many. On the facing page is a chart of basic tools you'll need to care for your new bed or border, with tips on how to use them. ❧

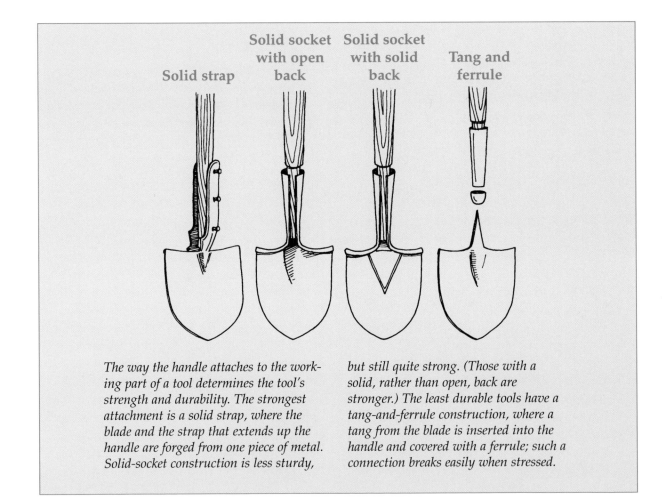

Solid strap   Solid socket with open back   Solid socket with solid back   Tang and ferrule

The way the handle attaches to the working part of a tool determines the tool's strength and durability. The strongest attachment is a solid strap, where the blade and the strap that extends up the handle are forged from one piece of metal. Solid-socket construction is less sturdy, but still quite strong. (Those with a solid, rather than open, back are stronger.) The least durable tools have a tang-and-ferrule construction, where a tang from the blade is inserted into the handle and covered with a ferrule; such a connection breaks easily when stressed.

Tool name	Description, Uses, and Benefits
Edger	Flat, half-moon-shaped blade on long handle; cuts through sod and removes grass from bed and border edges; prevents grass from invading plantings
Garden fork	Long-handled fork with three to five sturdy tines; turns garden soil; a loaded fork is lighter to lift than a loaded shovel
Garden rake	Long-handled rake with short, sturdy, metal tines; breaks up clods and smooths cultivated soil; saves effort and water; a raked bed is easy to plant, the fine texture of raked soil absorbs water efficiently
Hand shears	Scissors-like pruning tool; bypass or anvil models available; bypass shears have sharp, overlapping blades; anvil types have one sharp and one dull anvil blade; cuts twigs and branches up to $1/2$ in. thick; handy small pruners useful for snipping flowers and trimming damaged branches
Hand weeder	Asparagus knife has metal shaft with forked head; short-handled cultivator type has curved prongs; uproots perennial weeds; useful between close plants; inexpensive tool to root out weeds between plants
Hedge shears	Two-handled, scissors-like tool with 12- to 28-inch-long blades; cuts back perennials and grasses; shears formal hedges; faster than hand pruners for cutting back bushy perennials
Hoe or cultivator	Flat-bladed, long-handled tool; slices weed roots off below soil surface; aerates soil, breaks up crusty soil so that water can penetrate
Leaf rake	Long-handled rake with long, flexible, fanned tines; cleans up garden debris and leaves; removes disease- and pest-harboring debris; flexible tines won't damage lawn grass roots
"Leaky" hose	Hoses perforated or made of porous material that "leaks" water along the length of the hose; a water-saving way to irrigate plants
Loppers	Pruning shears with long handles; bypass or anvil types; provides leverage for cutting branches up to $1 1/2$ in. in diameter; cuts through thick branches with minimal effort
Pruning saw	Small, curved (sometimes folding) saw with a 10- to 14-in. blade, large teeth; saws through branches over 2 in. thick; large teeth cut on the pull stroke; makes deeper cuts with each stroke than a hand saw
Shovel	Digging tool with pointed, curved blade attached to long, straight handle; useful for digging planting holes and scooping soil amendments
Spade	Digging tool with flat, rectangular blade, medium-length handle, usually ending in a D-shaped grip; used to dig planting holes and edge plantings
Trowel	Digging tool with short-handled, narrow or wide blade; useful for digging small planting holes while kneeling

Design: Conni Cross

CHAPTER 3

PLANTINGS FOR PROPERTY BORDERS

The six designs presented in this chapter
offer a variety of choices for defining
the edges of your yard. Whether you prefer
complete privacy or would like to share
your new garden with the neighbors,
you will find something here to fill your needs.
A garden border planted along
the edges of a property not only
beautifies the landscape, but can serve
several practical purposes as well.
It can screen an unattractive view,
diminish ambient noise,
create a sense of privacy, keep people from
walking across your property, and provide
color on both sides of the property line.

Landscaping solutions need not be boring or unattractive. Here, a colorful mixed border acts as a privacy screen for this backyard and looks more appealing and friendlier than would a row of tall evergreens—the traditional choice for screening views.

BEFORE PLANTING ON A PROPERTY LINE

Before planting at or very close to your property line, make sure you know the exact locations of your property's boundaries. If you don't have a property survey, get a copy from your local building department, or hire a surveyor to do one.

You'll also need to find out about any local zoning regulations that may influence planting at your property line. Maximum fence height and distance of a planting from the curb are often regulated, as are plant heights under power lines and near street corners.

And while good fences do make good neighbors, it's also a friendly gesture to discuss your plans with your neighbors before proceeding with any landscaping along a shared property border.

CREATING PRIVACY

A front or backyard can be screened from view with a solid fence, dense plantings, or both. A fence provides instant privacy, while screen plantings take several years to fill in and do the job. However, a yard screened by shrubbery has a more relaxed, informal feel than a fenced yard. And any densely planted bed or border helps reduce noise better than a fence.

Siting a Private Garden

Siting a garden bed or border to create a sense of enclosure or to screen a view requires some forethought and a bit of reconnaissance work. Stroll around the perimeter of your property and view it from the sidewalk and from across the street. Try to look at your yard as a casual passerby would, and see what kind of views your current landscape offers. It may help to take a few snapshots to look at later.

Once you decide what you'd like to screen—whether it's a view of the street or your neighbor's backyard—site your new bed or border accordingly. It takes several

Carefully placed evergreen trees and shrubs screen the backyard of this corner property from the sidewalk and street. Perennials, bulbs, and groundcovers bring color throughout the growing season; a decorative fence provides interest as well as security for children and pets.

Design: Billie Gray

growing seasons to accomplish your goal, but your patience will be rewarded. For quicker results, buy larger specimens of the plants specified in the design.

Privacy Fences

By definition, a privacy fence must be at least 6 feet tall, so people can't see over it from the ground. (Blocking views from the second floor of a neighboring house is another matter, and may require careful placement of a tall tree or two.) If your zoning laws prohibit erecting a solid fence of 6 feet or taller, you can add plants to provide needed privacy. Or locate a taller fence away from the property border, along the side of a patio that needs screening, for instance.

Fences, especially solid ones, can look stark and unfriendly. Soften them with climbing vines or foreground plantings. And instead of solid bare boards, choose a louvered-style fence, or one made of closely spaced narrow boards—anything that adds texture to the fence and detracts from its solid look.

Screening with Plants

Hedges and tall screen plantings of evergreen trees and shrubs provide year-round privacy. Deciduous plants provide as much privacy during the growing season as evergreens, but when leafless, they won't do as good a job. This may not be important, however, if you don't use the yard in winter. A mixed border consisting of both evergreen and deciduous plants screens out views both to and from your yard, to create a lovely private setting.

A PRIVATE, YET FRIENDLY, YARD

If your aim is to create a quiet and peaceful haven away from noise and distracting views into neighboring properties, you can choose from four of the six designs in this chapter. The Privacy Berm, Fence-Line Planting, Privacy Border, and Colorful Evergreen Border are your best

Good fences do make good neighbors, but a solid board fence looks imposing and unattractive unless it is softened. Here, small flowering trees, shrubs, and flowers help soften a fence.

Design: Conni Cross

bets for creating the most private and quiet spaces in your backyard.

Many neighborhoods have a friendly hometown feeling about them, which is partially due to the flowers in the front yards. If you're interested in sharing your garden with the neighbors, either the Street-Side Cottage Garden or the Corner Property Planting would be perfect for you. These borders aren't meant to provide complete privacy. The sheer excitement of the plantings will, however, distract attention away from your house, because pedestrians and drivers alike will be focused on your beautiful garden.

All of the plans in this chapter offer creative bed and border designs that provide beautiful landscape solutions for the borders of your property. If creating privacy is one of your landscape goals, then one of the plans here is sure to offer a beautiful solution. ❦

This privacy planting gets a head-start on creating an effective screen by beginning with a berm, which gives young plants a height advantage.

Regional Plant Lists

Because climate and growing conditions vary greatly throughout North America, it is impossible to list here specific plants for this landscape plan that would thrive in all regions of the country. However, you can order a Blueprint Package for this plan containing a list of plants, selected by experts, for your region.

The six-page Blueprint Package features a large-size version of this Plan View, plus a detailed Plant and Materials List. It also includes an illustrated list of hundreds of landscape plants suited to your region, to use if you wish to make substitutions, as well as planting instructions and plant adaptation maps to ensure professional-looking results.

See page 157 to order your regionalized Blueprint Package.

PRIVACY BERM

THIS NATURALISTIC BERM is planted with a season-spanning design that can transform a suburban yard into a quiet haven. The berm rises to 3 feet high—tall enough to make you forget that your neighbor's yard lies just beyond. Staggered plantings cover the berm and create baffles that muffle sound, while the diverse mix of plants provides color and interest all year long.

Intended for a backyard, the berm allows you to enjoy the remaining lawn in privacy. Tall, berry-producing evergreens located at the top of the berm provide immediate screening, while perennials and bulbs, ornamental grasses, and small flowering trees at the front provide seasonal bursts of brilliance. A flowering groundcover on the berm helps hold the soil in place and makes a graceful transition between the slope of the berm and the flat lawn area.

Wherever you decide to site the berm, be sure to maintain the original grade of the yard at the property line, to avoid violating zoning regulations. Also, be sure to add a 2- to 3-inch-thick layer of mulch to help the slope retain moisture and to discourage weeds.

LANDSCAPE PLAN L309 SHOWN IN SPRING
DESIGNED BY MICHAEL J. OPISSO

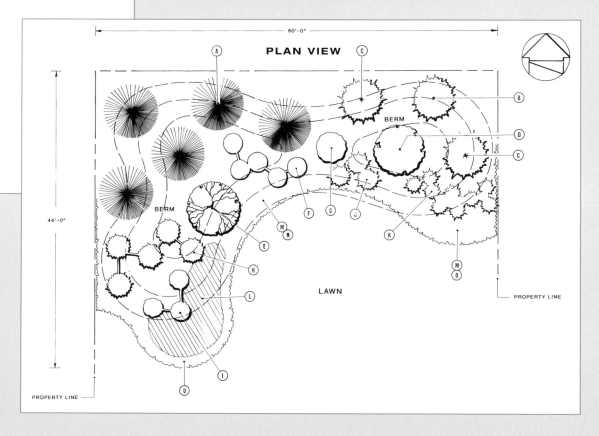

This design turns a necessary privacy or security fence into a landscape asset by softening it with vines and using it as a backdrop for a colorful garden.

Regional Plant Lists

Because climate and growing conditions vary greatly throughout North America, it is impossible to list here specific plants for this landscape plan that would thrive in all regions of the country. However, you can order a Blueprint Package for this plan containing a list of plants, selected by experts, for your region.

The six-page Blueprint Package features a large-size version of this Plan View, plus a detailed Plant and Materials List. It also includes an illustrated list of hundreds of landscape plants suited to your region, to use if you wish to make substitutions, as well as planting instructions and plant adaptation maps to ensure professional-looking results.

See page 157 to order your regionalized Blueprint Package.

FENCE-LINE PLANTING

THIS APPEALING BORDER is designed especially for a backyard that needs to be enclosed by a privacy fence. Here, the designer chooses a handsome fence to define the property line and provide screening, while creating a backdrop for a brilliant mixed border of sound-absorbing plants. The fence features a solid lower part that provides privacy and a lattice top that allows air to circulate and light to reach the garden. This design creates a healthier growing environment than a solid fence—and it's prettier, too.

The colorful planting softens the wooden fence behind it, enhancing rather than concealing it. Flowering vines, easily trained to grow on a fence, make a strong visual connection between the hardscape and softscape. Evergreens, perennials, bulbs, flowering shrubs, and vines all contribute color and interest throughout the year, while the fence provides a comforting sense of enclosure and permanence. The strategically placed groups of evergreens also provide additional privacy and help to anchor the design without obscuring the fence.

LANDSCAPE PLAN L310 SHOWN IN SPRING
DESIGNED BY DAMON SCOTT

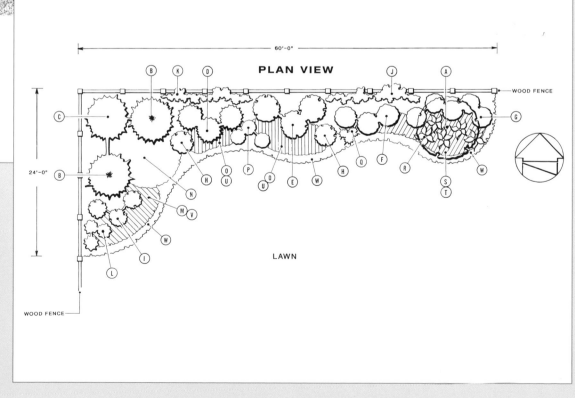

Here, a dense planting of assorted evergreens, set off by a changing show of flowering deciduous trees and shrubs, screens a neighboring property and effectively muffles noise.

Regional Plant Lists

Because climate and growing conditions vary greatly throughout North America, it is impossible to list here specific plants for this landscape plan that would thrive in all regions of the country. However, you can order a Blueprint Package for this plan containing a list of plants, selected by experts, for your region.

The six-page Blueprint Package features a large-size version of this Plan View, plus a detailed Plant and Materials List. It also includes an illustrated list of hundreds of landscape plants suited to your region, to use if you wish to make substitutions, as well as planting instructions and plant adaptation maps to ensure professional-looking results.

See page 157 to order your regionalized Blueprint Package.

PRIVACY BORDER

IF YOU'D LIKE TO CREATE A PRIVATE HAVEN in your back-yard without putting up a fence, this plan is for you. This backyard border relies solely on massed plantings of evergreen and deciduous trees and shrubs to screen out neighboring properties and to buffer noise. The designer also includes a charming circular bench where you can sit and enjoy a peaceful yard under the shade of a tree. Edged with flowering groundcovers and bulbs, the circular bed and the main border fit together naturally, like the pieces of a puzzle.

Starting with spring-flowering bulbs, this border design offers varied color and texture throughout the year. Broad-leaved and needle-leaved evergreens at the back of the border provide a permanent structure, effective screening, and a pleasantly neutral color that sets off the vibrant perennials and bulbs planted in front. The stepping-stones leading through the flowering groundcovers at the tree's base encourage visitors to meander across the lawn to get a closer look at the abundant plantings in the main border.

LANDSCAPE PLAN L311 SHOWN IN SPRING
DESIGNED BY JIM MORGAN

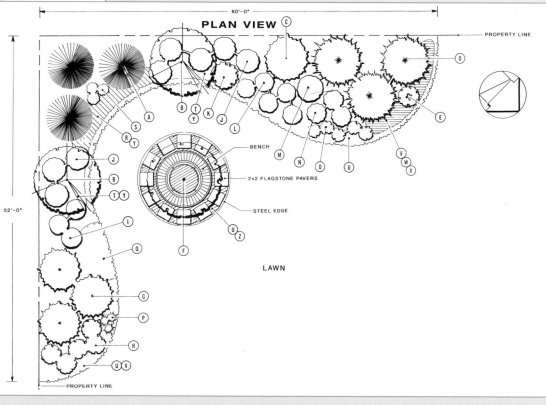

An attractive landscape along the edges of a corner property not only beautifies the neighborhood, but it goes a long way toward creating a peaceful setting where the house and yard have increased privacy from street traffic.

Regional Plant Lists

Because climate and growing conditions vary greatly throughout North America, it is impossible to list here specific plants for this landscape plan that would thrive in all regions of the country. However, you can order a Blueprint Package for this plan containing a list of plants, selected by experts, for your region.

The six-page Blueprint Package features a large-size version of this Plan View, plus a detailed Plant and Materials List. It also includes an illustrated list of hundreds of landscape plants suited to your region, to use if you wish to make substitutions, as well as planting instructions and plant adaptation maps to ensure professional-looking results.

See page 157 to order your regionalized Blueprint Package.

CORNER PROPERTY PLANTING

AN EXPANSIVE FRONT LAWN IS NICE if you live on a quiet, secluded lot, but on a busy corner lot, you'll need a more substantial planting to create privacy. This L-shaped bed effectively screens the front yard from the street, yet also allows visibility for traffic at both corners. And it looks just as good from the street side as it does from the yard side.

The designer chooses landscape plants that are all tough enough to retain their good looks despite the onslaught of car exhaust and road salt. Bulbs that will naturalize and spread, compact shrubs that won't need pruning, and tough perennials and pollution-resistant trees that aren't daunted by a difficult growing site put on a year-round show with minimal maintenance.

All you'll need to do is deadhead spent blossoms from time to time to encourage more flowers, and add mulch annually to control weeds and save on watering. Be sure to leave a wide mulched strip at the curb to allow maintenance access from the street side, leave the view open for drivers, and accommodate snow piles in cold-winter climates.

LANDSCAPE PLAN L312 SHOWN IN SUMMER
DESIGNED BY DAMON SCOTT

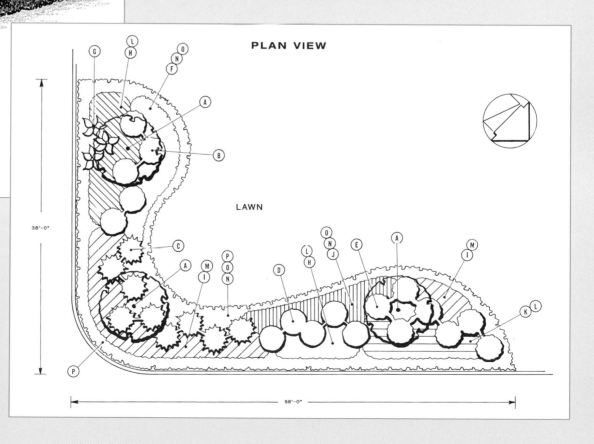

PLAN VIEW

LAWN

38'-0"

58'-0"

Colorful Evergreen Border

HERE'S A BORDER GARDEN MUCH RICHER in texture and color than most traditional evergreen hedgerows. Although evergreens are a common choice for defining private space because they provide year-round screening, their green color can be boring and monotonous. The designer overcomes that problem here by using many evergreen trees and shrubs that are available in shades of gold, blue, and green to create a luxuriant privacy border.

The various colors and textures of the foliage plants, which vary from feathery to bold, are skillfully combined to form a striking and harmonious composition. Unlike deciduous trees and shrubs, which put on a colorful but brief show, the evergreens that form the mainstay of this design hold their elegant jewel-toned colors all year. The evergreens also attract birds, which make nests in the dense, lush foliage and feast on the berries and cones.

An ever-changing show of bulbs, perennials, groundcovers, ornamental grasses, and flowering shrubs, placed at the border's front edge, stands out against the backdrop of evergreens. The border's free-form curves and natural shapes nicely balance the formality of a single clipped hedge.

LANDSCAPE PLAN L313 SHOWN IN SUMMER
DESIGNED BY GARY J. MARTIN

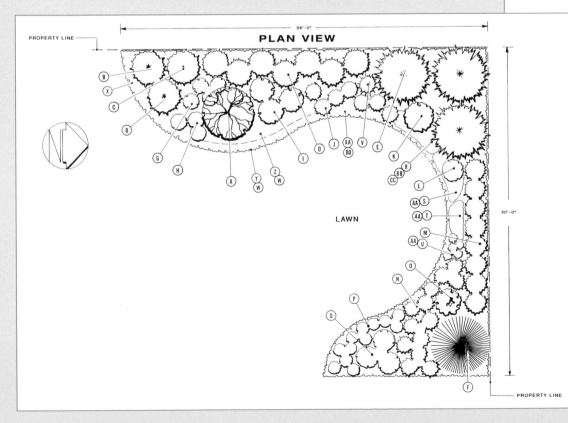

PLAN VIEW

PROPERTY LINE

56'-0"

LAWN

50'-0"

PROPERTY LINE

Regional Plant Lists

Because climate and growing conditions vary greatly throughout North America, it is impossible to list here specific plants for this landscape plan that would thrive in all regions of the country. However, you can order a Blueprint Package for this plan containing a list of plants, selected by experts, for your region.

The six-page Blueprint Package features a large-size version of this Plan View, plus a detailed Plant and Materials List. It also includes an illustrated list of hundreds of landscape plants suited to your region, to use if you wish to make substitutions, as well as planting instructions and plant adaptation maps to ensure professional-looking results.

See page 157 to order your regionalized Blueprint Package.

This privacy border relies on an assortment of evergreens with colorful needles to provide year-round screening while also creating a landscape scene that's always interesting to look at.

STREET-SIDE COTTAGE GARDEN

BURSTING WITH EXUBERANT OLD-FASHIONED blossoms, this friendly cottage garden is designed to be enjoyed from both sides of the fence. The garden invites passersby to pause and enjoy the show from the street or sidewalk, thus creating a homey neighborhood feeling. However, where space is very limited, you might prefer to plant only the inside of the fence and to plant the street side with a mowing strip of grass or a low-maintenance groundcover. You could even reverse the plan and install the hedge on the street side. If you live in a cold-winter climate, be sure to leave a buffer between the edge of the border and the street so there'll be room to pile snow.

Flowering perennial and annual climbing vines cover the wooden arbor, creating a romantic entrance. Roses, bulbs, perennials, annuals, and a compact evergreen hedge are arranged in a classic cottage-garden style that is casual but not haphazard. The designer achieves a pleasant sense of unity by repeating plants and colors throughout the design without repeating a symmetrical planting pattern. This helps create the casual feeling essential to a cottage garden.

LANDSCAPE PLAN L314 SHOWN IN SUMMER
DESIGNED BY MARIA MORRISON

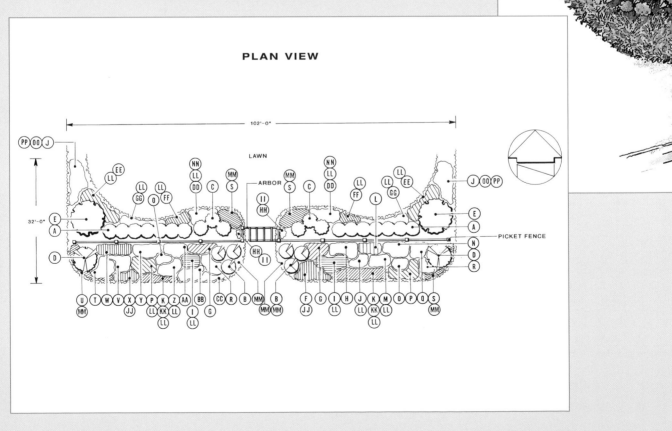

PLAN VIEW

Regional Plant Lists

Because climate and growing conditions vary greatly throughout North America, it is impossible to list here specific plants for this landscape plan that would thrive in all regions of the country. However, you can order a Blueprint Package for this plan containing a list of plants, selected by experts, for your region.

The six-page Blueprint Package features a large-size version of this Plan View, plus a detailed Plant and Materials List. It also includes an illustrated list of hundreds of landscape plants suited to your region, to use if you wish to make substitutions, as well as planting instructions and plant adaptation maps to ensure professional-looking results.

See page 157 to order your regionalized Blueprint Package.

See page 157 to order your regionalized Blueprint Package.

Create a friendly neighborhood feeling by planting this flower-filled cottage garden along the front of your property.

CHAPTER 4

DESIGNS FOR WATER–THRIFTY GARDENS

*The four plans in this chapter
are designed for sunny, exposed sites
where a more traditional garden
bed or border would suffer from the effects
of heat, sun, and fast-draining soil.
All four designs should be sited where they
will get full sun (at least six hours a day).
Homeowners in arid regions will find
these lovely water-thrifty gardens
particularly suitable. Consider installing
a water-thrifty garden even if you live
in a more temperate region—
you can conserve a valuable resource
and save money on your water bill, too.*

*Even a site where the soil is poor and the sun is hot can be turned into
a beautiful easy-care garden like this one, if you choose plants that
prefer those growing conditions. Gravel is appropriate for paths in
such a setting.*

NATURALLY WATER-THRIFTY

Watering a large, thirsty garden on a regular basis can be time-consuming and costly. Many people are coming to the realization that "xeriscape" and "naturalistic" gardens make environmental sense and are a responsible alternative to traditional styles that require high maintenance and excessive amounts of water. Xeriscaping—using plants that have low water requirements—is a great way to conserve water and still have a beautiful garden. And by choosing native plants—those that grow naturally in the wild in your region—you can reduce maintenance, because such plants are perfectly adapted to your growing conditions and climate.

WATERING WATER-THRIFTY GARDENS

Whether you live in a hot, dry climate, as in many parts of the West, or in a more temperate climate, as in the Northeast, your garden's varying water needs are important to consider. Your yard may have exposed, dry areas as well as shady, damp areas, and you'll need to water them accordingly.

To make sure you're watering correctly, push a stick into the soil in various places throughout your garden soon after you water: the soil should be dampened to a uniform depth of about 1 foot, deeper for most shrubs and trees. If the soil is drier in some places, adjust your watering system accordingly. You can also add more compost to particularly dry or fast-draining areas.

Although all four plans in this chapter are designed with water conservation in mind, don't assume that the plants will thrive without *some* water. Drought-tolerant plants are just that: they'll tolerate drought once established, but that doesn't mean they'll look their best without adequate amounts of water.

If rain is insufficient, it's especially important to provide water until the plants are thoroughly established. During the first few growing seasons, you'll probably need to water as often as you would any other planting. Once the plantings have taken a firm hold, you don't need to water regularly unless the summer is unusually dry. Then water deeply but infrequently—about once a week during particularly hot and dry periods.

To make watering even easier, consider installing a drip irrigation system, which you can operate with a timer. This type of system is especially convenient if you're away from home during the summer, when plants are more likely to suffer from excessive heat or drought. Drip irrigation delivers water directly to the plants' root system and doesn't waste water through evaporation.

SITING A WATER-THRIFTY GARDEN

The plans in this chapter make sense for just about any sunny garden spot—especially those hot spots

Xeriscape gardens are popular in the West, in areas where rainfall is scarce. These low-water-use plantings rely on drought-tolerant native plants, such as the pinyon pine, juniper, and California poppies used here. The lawn is native buffalo grass, which doesn't need irrigation.

Design: Jim Knopf

located next to a light-colored wall that reflects heat, or paved areas such as patios or driveways, which also hold and throw out a lot of drying heat. The plants are also particularly suitable for areas with sandy, fast-draining soil that dries out quickly.

Rather than surrounding your new water-thrifty bed or border with a thirsty lawn, consider a sea of natural-colored crushed stone or gravel. If you must have a lawn area, select an easy-care, drought-tolerant, turf-type fescue in the East or buffalo grass in the West.

CHOOSING A WATER-THRIFTY PLAN

Just because your garden is water-thrifty doesn't mean it has to be drab or monochromatic. In fact, many plants that thrive under less-than-ideal conditions have charms not found in more common garden plants, such as long-lasting flowers and silvery, scented, succulent, or furry leaves.

Many herbs that offer beautiful, scented flowers and leaves flourish in dry, exposed sites. The Herbal Island Bed design takes full advantage of the fragrance and casual habit of many herbs, and places them within a formal context of concentric circles. The other three plans in this chapter have a more casual style and feature diverse combinations of drought-tolerant perennials, bulbs, flowering shrubs, ornamental grasses, and evergreens.

You're sure to find at least one garden from among these four to suit your style and that of your home. The designs range from classic, as in the Herbal Island Bed, to naturalistic, as in both the Water-Wise Perennials and Naturalistic Flowers and Grasses, to Oriental, as in the Dry Streambed. And there's no shortage of color and texture in these plans. ❧

Many herbs, such as the lavender flanking this garden gate, hail from Mediterranean regions where the soil is poor and rainfall is light. They make pretty— and useful— additions to low-water-use gardens.

WATER-SAVING STRATEGIES

Try these strategies for reducing your garden's water needs:

- Mulch with organic materials such as wood chips, shredded bark, or leaves (see page 21).

- Select drought-tolerant plants.

- Improve the soil with well-rotted compost before planting.

- Reduce or eliminate lawns. Use low-maintenance groundcovers instead of lawns for a "green" look.

Because most herbs hail from the dry climate of the Mediterranean, an herb garden makes a practical, and pretty, solution for landscaping a site that features poor, dry soil.

Regional Plant Lists

Because climate and growing conditions vary greatly throughout North America, it is impossible to list here specific plants for this landscape plan that would thrive in all regions of the country. However, you can order a Blueprint Package for this plan containing a list of plants, selected by experts, for your region.

The six-page Blueprint Package features a large-size version of this Plan View, plus a detailed Plant and Materials List. It also includes an illustrated list of hundreds of landscape plants suited to your region, to use if you wish to make substitutions, as well as planting instructions and plant adaptation maps to ensure professional-looking results.

See page 157 to order your regionalized Blueprint Package.

HERBAL ISLAND BED

INSPIRED BY CLASSIC HERB GARDEN DESIGNS, this lovely circular island bed brims with water-thrifty culinary delights. Because many herbs demand excellent drainage, they are the perfect answer for a dry site. All the plants used here also need full sun, so locate the bed in the brightest part of your yard. A sundial placed at the design's center adds the perfect touch to the sunny location that herbs prefer.

The designer creates the circular structure of this bed with elegant dry-laid bluestone paths edged with low-growing evergreen shrubs. Herbs tend to have an informal, sprawling habit, which makes a pleasing contrast with the clean geometry of the circular paths and neatly clipped hedges. For a more casual effect, leave the hedges unsheared. You can also substitute another path material, such as brick-edged gravel or shredded mulch to match elements in your landscape.

Where space is limited, plant only the inner circle of the design. If you're short on time and money, consider planting the inner circle one year and the second circle the following year.

LANDSCAPE PLAN L315 SHOWN IN SUMMER
DESIGNED BY DAMON SCOTT

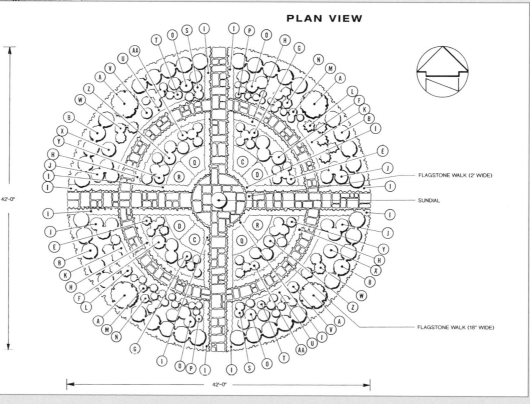

PLAN VIEW

FLAGSTONE WALK (2' WIDE)

SUNDIAL

FLAGSTONE WALK (18" WIDE)

42'-0"

42'-0"

Dry Streambed

Inspired by contemplative Oriental gardens, this naturalistic garden relies on boulders, a layer of gravel, and a slope of fieldstone to suggest the bed of a former stream. A simple wooden footbridge leads over the stream to a gazebo at the right edge of the bed. The design includes a lovely palette of shrubs, perennials, small trees, and ornamental grasses, all of which require minimal watering and, as an added bonus, are low-maintenance. This leaves you more time to spend in the gazebo meditating and contemplating your surroundings.

The bed, which can be located in any open area of your property, is dug to a depth of 6 feet. A layer of gravel lines the interior of the bed, giving it a natural appearance. The designer creates a berm on the upper side of the bed from the excavated soil. You may prefer to create a flatter design, digging instead to a depth of only 1 or 2 feet. Even this slight change in elevation is enough to create the desired effect of allowing the water-thrifty plants to flow over the banks and make a visual reference to a stream that is no longer there.

Landscape Plan L316 Shown in Summer
Designed by Michael J. Opisso

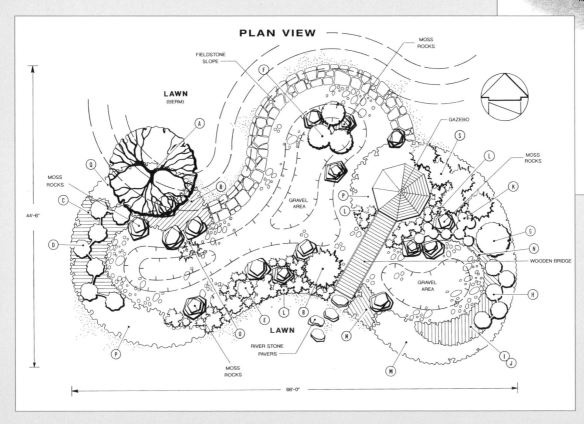

PLAN VIEW

MOSS ROCKS

FIELDSTONE SLOPE

LAWN (BERM)

MOSS ROCKS

GAZEBO

MOSS ROCKS

MOSS ROCKS

44'-6"

GRAVEL AREA

WOODEN BRIDGE

GRAVEL AREA

LAWN

RIVER STONE PAVERS

MOSS ROCKS

66'-0"

Regional Plant Lists

Because climate and growing conditions vary greatly throughout North America, it is impossible to list here specific plants for this landscape plan that would thrive in all regions of the country. However, you can order a Blueprint Package for this plan containing a list of plants, selected by experts, for your region.

The six-page Blueprint Package features a large-size version of this Plan View, plus a detailed Plant and Materials List. It also includes an illustrated list of hundreds of landscape plants suited to your region, to use if you wish to make substitutions, as well as planting instructions and plant adaptation maps to ensure professional-looking results.

See page 157 to order your regionalized Blueprint Package.

Pretty to look at and easy to care for, this garden features a rocky former streambed to complement the drought-tolerant plants.

Not all flowers need even moisture and rich soil to perform well. This design features a beautiful array of perennials that bloom prolifically in poor soil and drought conditions.

Regional Plant Lists

Because climate and growing conditions vary greatly throughout North America, it is impossible to list here specific plants for this landscape plan that would thrive in all regions of the country. However, you can order a Blueprint Package for this plan containing a list of plants, selected by experts, for your region.

The six-page Blueprint Package features a large-size version of this Plan View, plus a detailed Plant and Materials List. It also includes an illustrated list of hundreds of landscape plants suited to your region, to use if you wish to make substitutions, as well as planting instructions and plant adaptation maps to ensure professional-looking results.

See page 157 to order your regionalized Blueprint Package.

Water-Wise Perennials

Although dry, sunny sites can be challenging, it's possible to enjoy a lush, colorful garden even in areas of your yard with fast-draining, sandy soil and full-sun exposure. Place this three-pronged bed anywhere in your landscape that gets the full force of the sun. The garden will be sure to thrive, since the designer takes special care to select water-thrifty plants.

Once these water-wise perennials become established, you'll expend very little effort keeping them watered. Keep in mind, however, that even drought-tolerant perennials need to be well watered during the first year after planting. And during periods of extreme heat or prolonged drought, you'll probably need to water a bit more than usual.

This colorful garden is divided into three planting areas by two shredded-mulch paths. A wooden arbor over one path adds structure, provides a visual anchor, and creates interesting shadows as the sun passes overhead. Moss rocks create a second, stronger visual anchor and furnish a backdrop for the surrounding plants. The ornamental grasses and yuccas add height and a sense of balance to the composition.

Landscape Plan L317 Shown in Summer
Designed by patrick J. Duffe

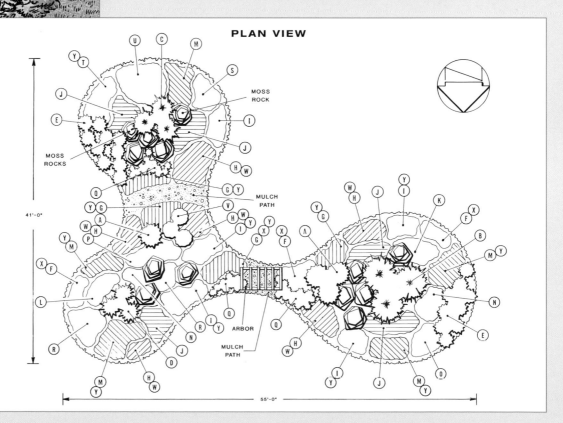

PLAN VIEW

MOSS ROCK

MOSS ROCKS

MULCH PATH

ARBOR

MULCH PATH

41'-0"

55'-0"

You won't be worrying about your gardening chores while sitting on this pretty patio—the flowers and ornamental grasses used here thrive in poor soil and low moisture.

Regional Plant Lists

Because climate and growing conditions vary greatly throughout North America, it is impossible to list here specific plants for this landscape plan that would thrive in all regions of the country. However, you can order a Blueprint Package for this plan containing a list of plants, selected by experts, for your region.

The six-page Blueprint Package features a large-size version of this Plan View, plus a detailed Plant and Materials List. It also includes an illustrated list of hundreds of landscape plants suited to your region, to use if you wish to make substitutions, as well as planting instructions and plant adaptation maps to ensure professional-looking results.

See page 157 to order your regionalized Blueprint Package.

NATURALISTIC
FLOWERS AND GRASSES

DESIGNED WITH THE FLOWER LOVER IN MIND, this oasis of flowers and grasses looks great all year. Bright flower colors during spring and summer are followed in fall by the pale, elegant flowers and seed heads of the ornamental grasses. The seed heads and foliage persist until the following spring, decorating the winter landscape with their delicate flower-like plumes and wheat-like fronds. Don't cut the dried grasses back to the ground until just before the new growing season begins, so you can enjoy them all winter.

The garden is formed from three connecting beds, with three paths leading into a central paved area between them. Flagstone pavers, which are interplanted with scented groundcover plants, lead into this central patio. A medium-sized deciduous tree in each bed shades the flagstones and puts on a brilliant show before dropping its leaves in fall. This allows you to add a table and chairs, so you can sit quietly and enjoy the trio of colorful garden beds. Be sure to site this lovely design so that the path is visible from a distance. That way, visitors will be tempted to come and enjoy the patio and surrounding plantings.

LANDSCAPE PLAN L318 SHOWN IN SUMMER
DESIGNED BY DAMON SCOTT

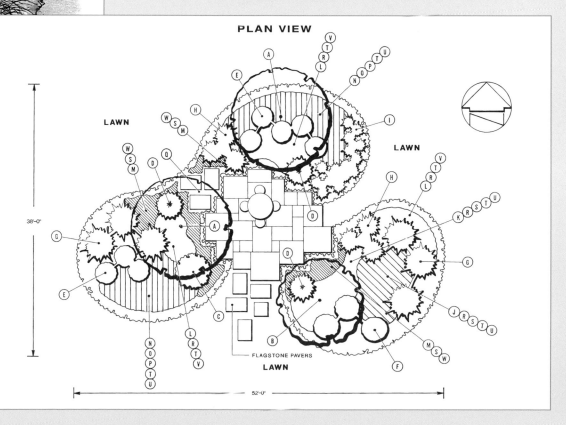

PLAN VIEW

LAWN

LAWN

LAWN

FLAGSTONE PAVERS

38'-0"

52'-0"

CHAPTER 5

GARDENS FOR FLOWER LOVERS

The five bed and border designs
featured in this chapter are sure
to capture the heart of any flower lover.
The plans contain a diverse selection
of flowering plants and range in style
from classic and traditional
to informal and naturalistic.
Every one of these plans works so
beautifully because their designers stuck to
the principles of good design.
When you design your own flower garden,
or modify any of these plans,
your chances of success will be greater
if you follow these same principles.

This flower border is effective because it follows basic design rules: the flowers are planted in masses and arranged by height, with the tallest in the background, mid-height ones in the mid-ground, and low, spreading types in the foreground.

STRUCTURAL ELEMENTS

A garden that focuses primarily on flowers needs some structure so that it looks good all the time. Many of the designs in this chapter use either hardscape structures, such as walls, fences, stepping stones, and arbors, or woody plants, such as trees and shrubs, to create a sense of permanence and year-round structure that flowers alone can't provide.

During the growing season, structural hardscape elements take a secondary role in a flower garden. In the colder months, when the leaves and flowers are gone, the structural elements of a design are more exposed and therefore more dominant, so it's important to consider their individual visual impact. For example, a ramshackle garden shed may look wonderfully charming when it's covered by the blossoms of a rose. However, it may look shabby in the winter, when the stems of the rose are completely bare.

HEDGES

A sheared evergreen hedge—either a tall one or a very low one—is a traditional way to create a permanent framework for a garden bed or border. Yew, boxwood, and Japanese holly are common choices. For a more casual effect, prune the hedge naturally instead of shearing it. You might even wish to add a few compact evergreens to the main garden and allow them to assume their natural, unpruned shape to add year-round greenery.

GRASSES

Tall ornamental grasses, added here and there in a garden bed, also make effective structural elements. Although they are herbaceous plants that die back to the ground, their dried foliage and light-catching seed heads stand throughout winter, adding a pretty note and a lot of volume to the winter garden. Tall grasses also add height to a border or bed of shorter perennials.

SMALL, DELICATE PERENNIALS

These plants create a cloud-like effect with their fine-textured foliage or their diminutive, delicate flowers that seem to float above the ground. Punctuate drifts of these airy perennials with more substantial plants to provide structure and anchor the design.

anemone (*Anemone sylvestris*)
astilbe (*Astilbe* x *hybrida*)
baby's breath (*Gypsophila paniculata*)
coreopsis (*Coreopsis verticillata* 'Moonbeam')
fennel (*Foeniculum vulgare* 'Purpureum')
forget-me-not (*Myosotis sylvatica*)
fringed bleeding heart (*Dicentra eximia*)
lavender mist (*Thalictrum rochebrunianum*)
perennial flax (*Linum perenne*)
white gaura (*Gaura lindheimeri*)
yellow corydalis (*Corydalis lutea*)

BIG, BOLD PERENNIALS

These perennials are characterized by their boldness—in the size and texture of the leaves, the soaring height of the flower stalks or the entire plant, the striking flowers, or a combination of these traits. Use these sparingly, for drama.

agave (*Agave parryi*) 🌿 ↕ ❀
caladium (*Caladium* x *hortulanum*) 🌿
cardoon (*Cynara cardunculus*) 🌿 ↕ ❀
flax (*Phormium tenax*) 🌿 ↕
giant ornamental onion (*Allium giganteum*) ❀
Joe-Pye weed (*Eupatorium fistulosum*) ↕ ❀
red hot poker (*Kniphofia uvaria*) ❀
shining coneflower (*Rudbeckia nitida*) 🌿 ↕ ❀
spiny bear's breeches (*Acanthus mollis*) 🌿 ↕ ❀
yucca (*Yucca filamentosa*) 🌿 ↕ ❀

🌿 bold leaf
↕ lofty height
❀ striking flower

TREES

Small ornamental trees such as stewartia, dogwood, and crabapple not only bring a dramatic spring floral show and fall foliage color to a garden, but also add height, creating a three-dimensional effect. They cast a bit of shade beneath their boughs, creating a place to grow favorite shade-loving perennials. Deciduous shrubs have the same effect, though on a smaller scale.

COMBINING FLOWERS AND FOLIAGE

Try to contrast flower shapes and colors so the garden doesn't become monotonous. Plant large groups of one kind of flower next to a drift of another type, and be sure each group has a different flower shape, texture,

Artfully combining plants is the key to designing a successful bed or border. Here, catmint's upright spires make a pretty contrast to cranesbill's round blossoms. The pastel colors are pleasing, too.

Design: Kristin Horne

SPIRELIKE PERENNIALS FOR VERTICAL EFFECTS

Use these and other tall perennials where you want to add a vertical element to a design; contrast them with mounded or rounded plants.

cardinal flower *(Lobelia cardinalis)*
delphinium *(Delphinium* hybrids)
foxglove *(Digitalis purpurea)*
hybrid sage *(Salvia* x *superba)*
lupine *(Lupinus* hybrids*)*
monkshood *(Aconitum* spp.*)*
mullein *(Verbascum* x *hybridum)*
Russian sage *(Perovskia atriplicifolia)*
veronica *(Veronica spicata)*

or color. Contrast daisy shapes, lily shapes, globes, and spikes for an engaging, lively, balanced design. Plant bold-textured plants with delicate plants, and be sure to avoid hiding short plants behind tall ones.

Foliage texture and color are as important as flower shapes and colors. For continuity and a visual break from the colors of flowers, choose foliage plants to separate drifts of flowers. Contrast the airiness of fine-textured ferns, for instance, with the solidity of large-leaved hostas to create a lively scene. Add a cluster of purple-leaf coral-bells or gold-leaf hostas, and you'll enjoy their color for many months. ❧

OLD-FASHIONED ROSES AND PERENNIALS

A ROMANTIC OLD-FASHIONED ROSE BORDER is always in style. The voluptuous fragrance and heavy-petaled blossoms of roses bring charm to any sunny garden. Here, the designer chooses old garden roses, which offer scent as well as ease of care, unlike modern hybrid tea roses. Although many of these cherished plants bloom only once during the season, their other charms far outweigh the repeat-blossoms of their modern cousins. Many have excellent summer and fall foliage and a heavy crop of glossy rose hips in autumn.

In this border design, these belles of the garden are mixed with classic perennial partners and bulbs to create months of color and interest. A circular bed is tucked into this pleasingly curved border and is separated by a ribbon-like strip of lawn. A rose-covered pergola frames a classically inspired sculpture in the border's center, creating two balanced focal points. A stone bench placed under the arbor provides a lovely spot to contemplate the wonders of this flower-filled haven. Mulched pathways at the back of the border allow easy access for maintenance and for cutting flowers for the house.

LANDSCAPE PLAN L319 SHOWN IN SUMMER
DESIGNED BY MARIA MORRISON

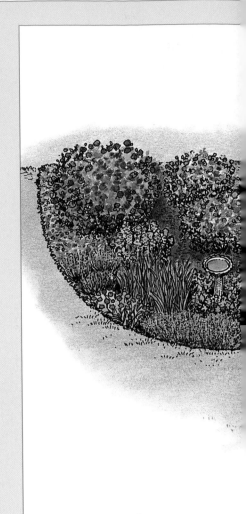

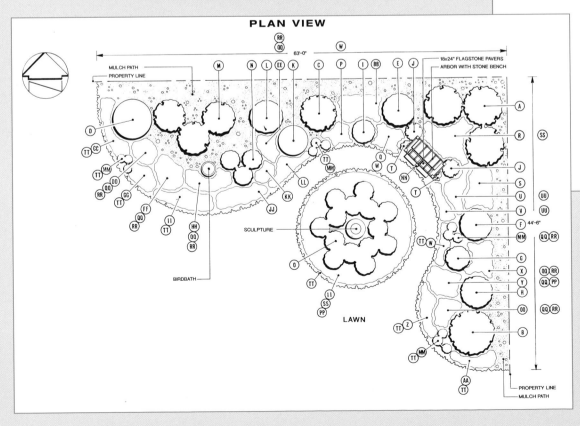

PLAN VIEW

MULCH PATH
PROPERTY LINE
63'-0"
18x24" FLAGSTONE PAVERS
ARBOR WITH STONE BENCH
44'-6"
SCULPTURE
BIRDBATH
LAWN
PROPERTY LINE
MULCH PATH

Regional Plant Lists

Because climate and growing conditions vary greatly throughout North America, it is impossible to list here specific plants for this landscape plan that would thrive in all regions of the country. However, you can order a Blueprint Package for this plan containing a list of plants, selected by experts, for your region.

The six-page Blueprint Package features a large-size version of this Plan View, plus a detailed Plant and Materials List. It also includes an illustrated list of hundreds of landscape plants suited to your region, to use if you wish to make substitutions, as well as planting instructions and plant adaptation maps to ensure professional-looking results.

See page 157 to order your regionalized Blueprint Package.

Designed to beautify the corner of a backyard, this rose-filled border can easily be turned into a free-standing bed for the center of a lawn: simply round off the straight sides into a more free-flowing shape.

A curving stone retaining wall and small flowering tree give this flower garden dimension and form, which keeps it attractive throughout the year.

Regional Plant Lists

Because climate and growing conditions vary greatly throughout North America, it is impossible to list here specific plants for this landscape plan that would thrive in all regions of the country. However, you can order a Blueprint Package for this plan containing a list of plants, selected by experts, for your region.

The six-page Blueprint Package features a large-size version of this Plan View, plus a detailed Plant and Materials List. It also includes an illustrated list of hundreds of landscape plants suited to your region, to use if you wish to make substitutions, as well as planting instructions and plant adaptation maps to ensure professional-looking results.

See page 157 to order your regionalized Blueprint Package.

RAISED FLOWER BED

A COLORFUL, EASY-CARE FLOWER BED like this paisley-shaped raised bed can be located almost anywhere on your property—it is perfectly suitable as an entry garden, or as a transition between different levels in a backyard. The bed's curving, organic shape echoes the sinuous stone wall that divides its upper and lower sections. Flagstone steps further divide the bed and lead visitors from the lower, more symmetrical area to the upper, more asymmetrical section of the garden.

The designer arranges lovely, low-growing flowering perennials to spill over the wall, creating a curtain of flowers. Twin flowering shrubs flank the entry steps, while a single specimen of the same type marks the exit. The rest of the bed is planted with a profusion of easy-care perennials, bulbs, ornamental grasses, and flowering shrubs.

This garden bed requires only a little of your precious time for routine maintenance. You'll need to remove spent blossoms, do a bit of cleanup in spring and fall, and divide the perennials every few years.

LANDSCAPE PLAN L320 SHOWN IN SUMMER
DESIGNED BY SALVATORE A. MASULLO

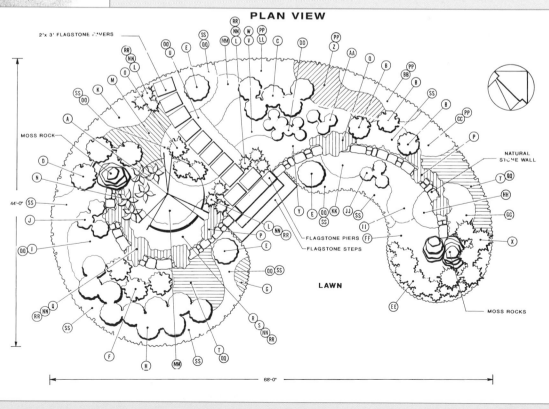

PLAN VIEW

2'x 3' FLAGSTONE PAVERS

MOSS ROCK

44'-0"

NATURAL STONE WALL

FLAGSTONE PIERS
FLAGSTONE STEPS

LAWN

MOSS ROCKS

68'-0"

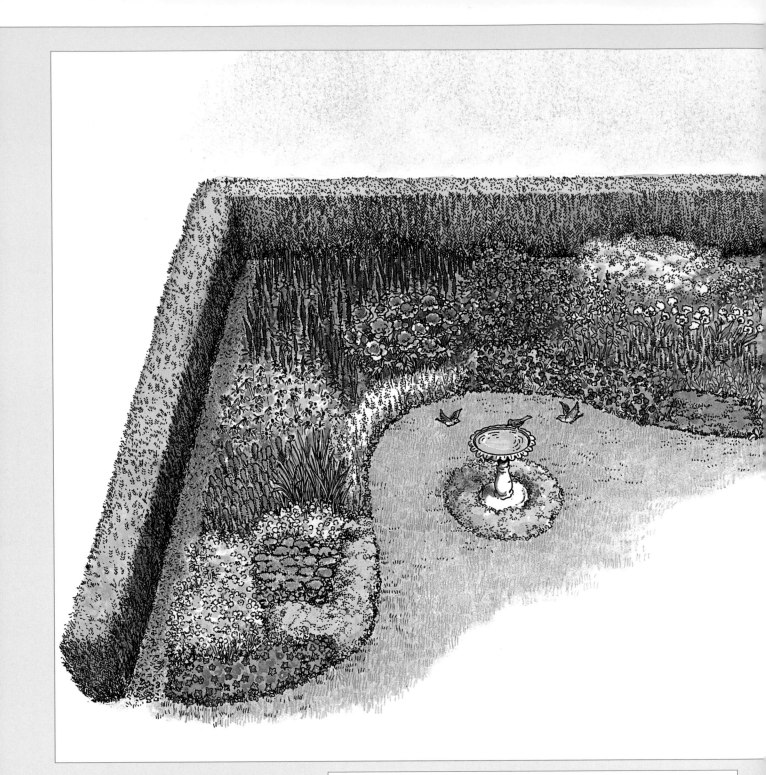

The English perennial border with its graceful masses of ever-changing flowers represents the epitome of fine perennial gardening. Planted in a corner of your property, this garden will provide enjoyment for years to come, since the designer filled it with an array of long-lasting, hardy plants.

Regional Plant Lists

Because climate and growing conditions vary greatly throughout North America, it is impossible to list here specific plants for this landscape plan that would thrive in all regions of the country. However, you can order a Blueprint Package for this plan containing a list of plants, selected by experts, for your region.

The six-page Blueprint Package features a large-size version of this Plan View, plus a detailed Plant and Materials List. It also includes an illustrated list of hundreds of landscape plants suited to your region, to use if you wish to make substitutions, as well as planting instructions and plant adaptation maps to ensure professional-looking results.

See page 157 to order your regionalized Blueprint Package.

ENGLISH PERENNIAL BORDER

THE BRITISH, BEING RENOWNED GARDENERS, boast the prettiest flower gardens in the world. Their success in growing perennials to perfection partly lies in the amenable British climate—cool summers, mild winters, and plenty of moisture all year. Even without a perfect climate, you can achieve the epitome of a perennial garden in your own backyard by using plants well-adapted to your climate and arranging them in the flowing drifts typical of English gardens.

This perennial border fits nicely into a corner of almost any sunny yard. Pictured here with a traditional evergreen hedge as a backdrop, the garden looks equally lovely in front of a fence or house wall, as long as the area receives at least six hours of full sun a day. The designer carefully selects an assortment of spring-, summer-, and fall-blooming perennials, arranging them in artful drifts for an ever-changing display. Spring and summer blossoms paint a delightful pink, magenta, and pale yellow color scheme enlivened here and there with splashes of white and blue, while autumn brings deeper colors—gold, dark pink, and purple. Patches of burgundy- and silver-hued foliage in the foreground play up the flower colors.

LANDSCAPE PLAN L276 SHOWN IN SUMMER
DESIGNED BY MICHAEL J. OPISSO

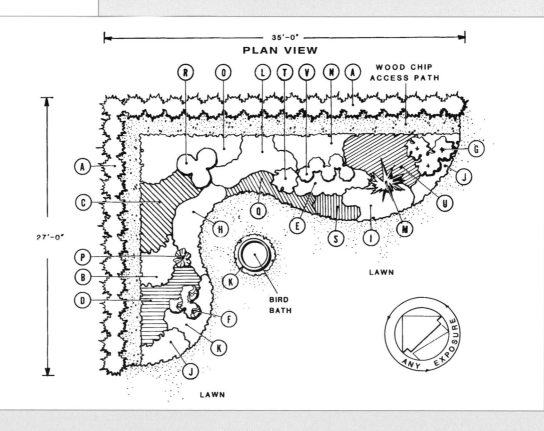

Natural color companions, blue and yellow flowers create a pleasing garden scene that looks great any where it's planted. This island bed works perfectly in an open sunny yard, but could be modified to fit along the side of a house or to back up against a fence or hedge along a property border.

Regional Plant Lists

Because climate and growing conditions vary greatly throughout North America, it is impossible to list here specific plants for this landscape plan that would thrive in all regions of the country. However, you can order a Blueprint Package for this plan containing a list of plants, selected by experts, for your region.

The six-page Blueprint Package features a large-size version of this Plan View, plus a detailed Plant and Materials List. It also includes an illustrated list of hundreds of landscape plants suited to your region, to use if you wish to make substitutions, as well as planting instructions and plant adaptation maps to ensure professional-looking results.

See page 157 to order your regionalized Blueprint Package.

BLUE-AND-YELLOW ISLAND BED

BLUE AND YELLOW FLOWERS planted together reward the gardener with a color scheme that's as bright and pretty as any garden can be. It's hard to err when using these colors, because the pure blues and the lavender blues—whether dark or pastel—look just as pretty with the pale lemon yellows as with the bright sulfur yellows and the golden yellows. Each combination makes a different statement—subtle and sweet, as with the pastels, or bold and demanding, as with the deep vivid hues. But no combination fails to please.

The designer of this beautiful island bed, which can be situated in any sunny spot, effectively orchestrates a sequence of blue and yellow perennials to bloom from spring through fall. And the designer incorporates various shapes and textures to make a happy composition. Fluffy, rounded flower heads set off elegant spires, while mounded shapes mask lanky stems of taller plants. Although the garden's unmistakable color scheme is blue and yellow, an occasional spot of orange creates an exciting jolt of bright contrast. A few masses of creamy-white flowers frost the garden, easing stronger colors into a compatible union.

LANDSCAPE PLAN L278 SHOWN IN SUMMER
DESIGNED BY DAMON SCOTT

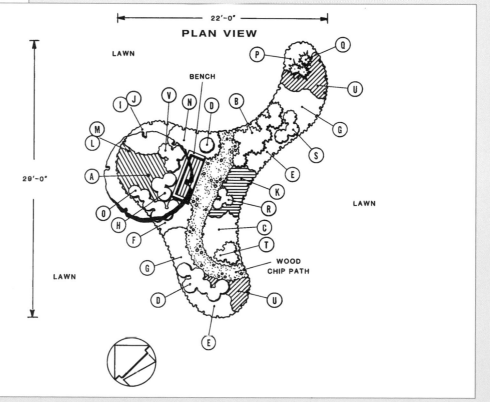

PLAN VIEW

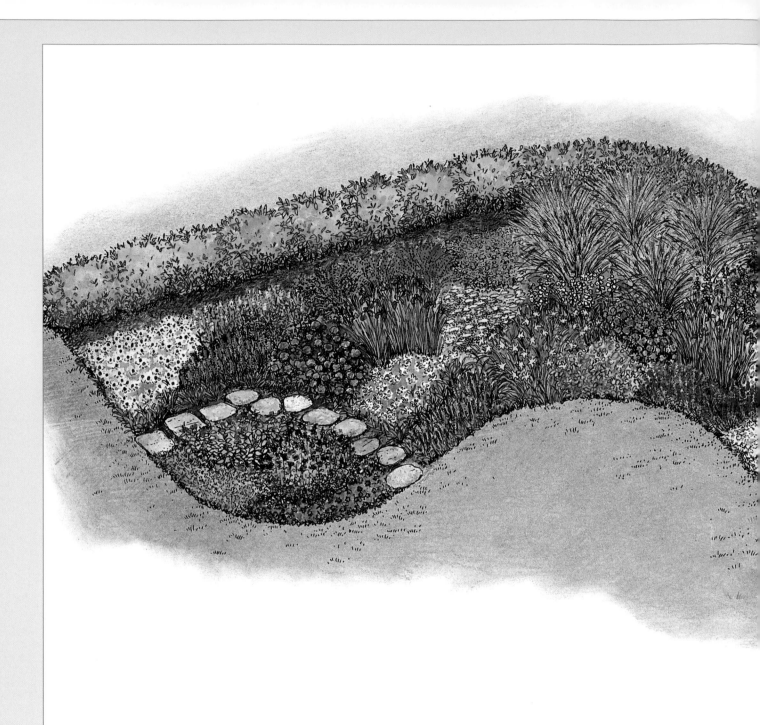

This bed brims with flower color from spring through fall, so be sure to site it in a sunny location where you can enjoy the scene from both indoors and out.

Regional Plant Lists

Because climate and growing conditions vary greatly throughout North America, it is impossible to list here specific plants for this landscape plan that would thrive in all regions of the country. However, you can order a Blueprint Package for this plan containing a list of plants, selected by experts, for your region.

The six-page Blueprint Package features a large-size version of this Plan View, plus a detailed Plant and Materials List. It also includes an illustrated list of hundreds of landscape plants suited to your region, to use if you wish to make substitutions, as well as planting instructions and plant adaptation maps to ensure professional-looking results.

See page 157 to order your regionalized Blueprint Package.

SEASON-SPANNING PERENNIAL GARDEN

IF YOU'D LIKE TO HAVE AN EASY-CARE GARDEN that offers more than a single burst of brilliant color, this season-spanning border packed with perennials is perfect for you. The designer selects a wide array of perennials that begin flowering in the spring, provide plenty of color throughout the summer, and continue blooming into the fall. All you'll need to do is remove spent blossoms from time to time and divide plants every few years.

A deciduous hedge curves around the back of the border, providing a pleasant foil for the perennials throughout the growing season. Before dropping its leaves in autumn, the hedge puts on its own show of dazzling color just as the perennials are beginning to slow down. Once the perennials have finished blooming, you can leave the dried flower heads on the plants to add subtle beauty to the winter landscape.

The classic curved shape of this border will fit easily into a corner of your front or backyard. If you have a large yard, you may want to install this border on one side with its mirror image on the other and with a path set between them.

LANDSCAPE PLAN L321 SHOWN IN SUMMER
DESIGNED BY MARIA MORRISON

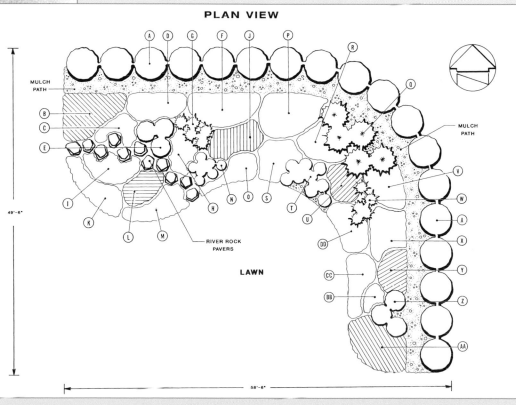

PLAN VIEW

MULCH PATH

MULCH PATH

RIVER ROCK PAVERS

LAWN

49'-6"

58'-6"

CHAPTER 6

DESIGNS FOR WEEKEND GARDENERS

*You may be a weekend gardener
because you're too busy during the week
to do more than sniff a flower or two
on your way out the front door.
Or you may have a weekend vacation home
that cries out for a garden that can
survive your absence during the work week.
Whatever your circumstances,
the easy-care designs in this chapter
may be the answer to your prayers.
They are designed with work-saving
strategies in mind and emphasize plants
that flourish with minimal attention,
so you can enjoy a delightful display
of flowers or a healthy harvest of herbs
with little effort on your part.*

It's possible to have a garden as colorful as this one with very little work. The secret is to use easy-care native plants, annuals that don't need deadheading, and hardy, pest-free shrubs.

EASY-CARE TIPS

Some gardens need more care than others. Here are some strategies you can use to create a reasonably low-maintenance garden:

✓ Site beds and borders close to the house so you can spend more time enjoying them and less time hauling garden tools to far-flung areas. As you have more time to garden, expand into the outer reaches of your yard.

✓ Install slow-growing or dwarf varieties of ornamental shrubs. That way, you won't have to prune to keep them within bounds.

✓ Mulch, mulch, mulch. Apply organic material (for example, wood chips, shredded leaves, well-rotted manure, or compost) to exposed garden soil to smother weeds, conserve water, and provide valuable nutrients to the soil.

✓ Install a drip irrigation system on a timer so plants won't dry out and perish while you're away.

✓ Install permanent edgings or mowing strips between the lawn and garden beds and borders to eliminate the need to trim lawn edges and to prevent grass from invading and becoming a problem.

✓ Use disease-resistant, long-lived, undemanding perennials and ornamental trees and shrubs instead of high-maintenance annuals or finicky, exotic plants. That way, you'll reduce the need to prune, stake, and pest-proof your garden.

SMART PLANT CHOICES

Shrink your list of garden chores by choosing plants that are suitable for your site. As obvious as this may sound, it's all too easy to fall in love with a high-maintenance hybrid tea rose when you'd be much better off choosing a gorgeous, easy-care shrub rose, such as a rugosa or a Meidiland hybrid. Instead of letting your affection for a particular plant guide your design decisions, think first about your growing conditions, the available space in your garden, and the time you're able to devote to its care. Then choose wisely.

Whatever conditions your garden offers—from hot, dry, blazing sun to cool, moist, shade—there are many plants that will thrive there. For example, if you're fond of shade-loving azaleas but live in a hot, dry climate, consider planting one of the Nuccio Hybrid azaleas that are bred to tolerate conditions that other azaleas can't abide.

Often, you can tell what conditions a plant prefers just by looking at it. For example, many plants that tolerate the hot, dry conditions of arid climates, as well as the salt spray and drying winds of seaside climates, have silvery, succulent, or woolly leaves, such as artemisia, yucca, and lamb's-ears. Silvery leaves reflect the sometimes punishing blaze of the sun. Succulent leaves store water that's handy during extended dry periods. Woolly leaves help conserve moisture and keep salt off. On the other end of the adaptability spectrum are plants that thrive in shade. Many of these, including hostas and ivy, have large, shiny, often dark-colored leaves that gather light.

One way to design an eye-catching, low-maintenance garden is to rely on colorful foliage plants. These ever-greens feature golden needles that bring a sunny glow to the garden, especially when juxtaposed against dark green plants.

Natives Versus Exotics

Plants that are native to your particular region are usually the easiest to care for, because they're completely adapted to whatever the region naturally supplies in the way of rainfall and soil conditions. (In fact, many wildflowers will die if subjected to the overzealous care of a gardener armed with a garden hose and fertilizer.) Non-native, or exotic, plants may also grow well in North American regions similar to their own natural habitats. For example, many Australian, African, and Mediterranean natives are perfectly suited to the hot, dry, desert-like conditions of southern California.

Deciding on a Style

"Easy-care" doesn't mean sloppy. You can create a formal look using low-maintenance plants. Topiary hedges and beds filled entirely with annuals that are common in formal gardens have no place in an easy-care landscape. Instead, you can achieve a formal but easy-care effect by installing a mass planting of a single type of summer-blooming perennials, interplanted with spring-blooming bulbs against a handsome brick or stone wall. Or, if you prefer a more casual look, you can plant mixed beds or borders using an informal, natural hedge as a backdrop. ❧

UNDEMANDING PLANTS FOR WEEKEND GARDENERS

This list of plants includes annuals that don't need deadheading to promote reblooming; unfussy, long-lasting flowering perennials; dependable bulbs that return every year; good-looking, non-invasive groundcovers; and handsome hedge plants that need minimal pruning.

Annuals
cleome (*Cleome hasslerana*)
creeping zinnia (*Sanvitalia procumbens*)
edging lobelia (*Lobelia erinus*)
impatiens (*Impatiens wallerana*)
Madagascar periwinkle (*Catharanthus roseus*)
sweet alyssum (*Lobularia maritima*)

Perennials
coneflower (*Rudbeckia fulgida*)
daylily (*Hemerocallis* hybrids and cultivars)
English lavender (*Lavandula angustifolia*)
fernleaf yarrow (*Achillea filipendulina*)
lady's mantle (*Alchemilla mollis*)
peony (*Paeonia lactiflora*)

Bulbs
crocus (*Crocus* x *vernus*)
daffodil (*Narcissus* cultivars)
glory-of-the-snow (*Chionodoxa luciliae*)
grape hyacinth (*Muscari armeniacum*)
snowdrop (*Galanthus nivalis*)
summer snowflake (*Leucojum aestivum*)

Groundcovers
big blue lilyturf (*Liriope muscari*)
creeping juniper (*Juniperus horizontalis*)
creeping thyme (*Thymus serpyllum*)
epimedium (*Epimedium* spp.)
lungwort (*Pulmonaria angustifolia*)
myrtle (*Vinca minor*)
woolly thyme (*Thymus pseudolanuginosus*)

Deciduous Hedge Plants
bridalwreath (*Spiraea* x *vanhouttei*)
Japanese barberry (*Berberis thunbergii*)
privet (*Ligustrum* spp.)
rugosa rose (*Rosa rugosa*)

Evergreen Hedge Plants
boxwood (*Buxus sempervirens* 'Suffruticosa')
Japanese holly (*Ilex crenata* 'Helleri')
yew (*Taxus baccata* 'Nana' and 'Repandens')

Brimming with easy-care flowers from spring through fall, this low-maintenance flower border evokes the spirit of an English garden, but doesn't need a staff to take care of it.

Regional Plant Lists

Because climate and growing conditions vary greatly throughout North America, it is impossible to list here specific plants for this landscape plan that would thrive in all regions of the country. However, you can order a Blueprint Package for this plan containing a list of plants, selected by experts, for your region.

The six-page Blueprint Package features a large-size version of this Plan View, plus a detailed Plant and Materials List. It also includes an illustrated list of hundreds of landscape plants suited to your region, to use if you wish to make substitutions, as well as planting instructions and plant adaptation maps to ensure professional-looking results.

See page 157 to order your regionalized Blueprint Package.

EASY-CARE ENGLISH BORDER

A FLOWER-FILLED GARDEN created in the romantic style of an English border need not demand much care, as this lovely design illustrates. The designer carefully selects unfussy bulbs and perennials, and a few flowering shrubs, all of which are disease- and insect-resistant, noninvasive, and don't need staking or other maintenance. A balance of spring-, summer-, and fall-blooming plants keeps the border exciting throughout the growing season.

Because English gardens are famous for their gorgeous roses, the designer includes several rosebushes, but chooses ones unharmed by bugs and mildew. Hedges form a backdrop for most English flower gardens; the designer plants an informal one here to reduce pruning. A generous mulched path runs between the flowers and the hedge, so it's easy to tend them, while the edging keeps grass from invading and creating a nuisance.

Plant this border along any sunny side of your property. Imagine it along the back of the yard, where you can view it from a kitchen window or from a patio or deck, along one side of the front yard, or planted with the hedge bordering the front lawn and providing privacy from the street.

LANDSCAPE PLAN L306 SHOWN IN SUMMER
DESIGNED BY MARIA MORRISON

PLAN VIEW

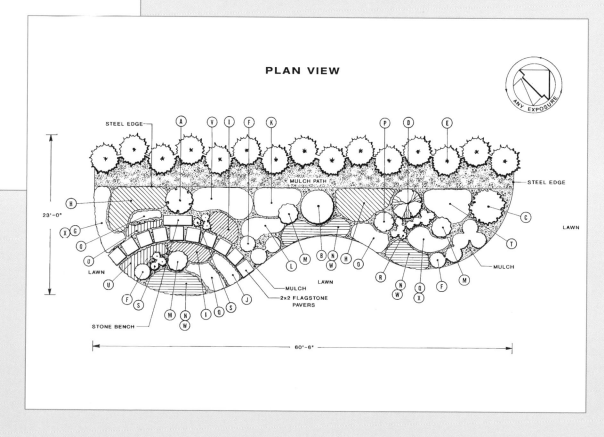

An herb garden fenced in cottage-garden style and located just off the back door is both attractive and practical.

Regional Plant Lists

Because climate and growing conditions vary greatly throughout North America, it is impossible to list here specific plants for this landscape plan that would thrive in all regions of the country. However, you can order a Blueprint Package for this plan containing a list of plants, selected by experts, for your region.

The six-page Blueprint Package features a large-size version of this Plan View, plus a detailed Plant and Materials List. It also includes an illustrated list of hundreds of landscape plants suited to your region, to use if you wish to make substitutions, as well as planting instructions and plant adaptation maps to ensure professional-looking results.

See page 157 to order your regionalized Blueprint Package.

DOORYARD
HERB GARDEN

DESIGNED IN THE STYLE OF OLD-FASHIONED dooryard gardens, this modern adaptation brings useful, edible plants within easy reach of your house. Site these beds and borders near the kitchen door so you'll have easy access to their bounty when cooking. Or move the entire garden to the center of a sunny lawn.

A herringbone-patterned brick walkway along one side of the garden guides you to one of the two entry gates. Mulched paths and irregular flagstones, interplanted with a scented, mat-forming groundcover, define the beds and borders. A picturesque wooden fence enclosing the entire garden provides a sense of structure, while its rectilinear form is echoed and softened by hedge plantings. If your space is limited, you might eliminate one or both of the hedges, the fence, or all of the hard- and softscape elements outside the garden beds.

The only maintenance tasks required involve harvesting, occasional cleanup, and replacing the annual herbs each year. You'll also need to refresh the mulch every year to prevent weeds from sprouting and to keep the beds neat.

LANDSCAPE PLAN L322 SHOWN IN SUMMER
DESIGNED BY SALVATORE A. MASULLO

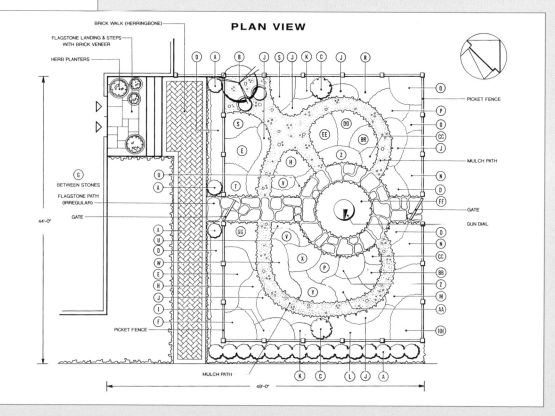

PLAN VIEW

BRICK WALK (HERRINGBONE)
FLAGSTONE LANDING & STEPS WITH BRICK VENEER
HERB PLANTERS
BETWEEN STONES
FLAGSTONE PATH (IRREGULAR)
GATE
44'-0"
PICKET FENCE
MULCH PATH
49'-0"

PICKET FENCE
MULCH PATH
GATE
SUN DIAL

Easy-Care
Mixed Border

When small trees, flowering shrubs, perennials, and groundcovers are planted together, the result is a lovely mixed border that looks great throughout the year. The trees and shrubs—both evergreen and deciduous types—provide structure and form in winter, while also offering decorative foliage and flowers in other seasons. Perennials and bulbs occupy large spaces between groups of woody plants, and contribute leaf texture and floral color to the scene.

Even though this border contains a lot of plants, it is easy to care for. That's part of the beauty of a mixed border—the woody plants are long-lived and need little pruning if allowed to grow naturally. By limiting the number of perennials and blanketing the ground with weed-smothering groundcovers, maintenance is kept to a minimum without sacrificing beauty.

You can install this mixed border in a sunny location almost anywhere on your property, though it's intended to run along the back of an average-sized lot. If your property is larger or smaller than the one in this plan, you can alter the design by either increasing or decreasing the number of plants in each grouping.

Landscape Plan L307 Shown in Spring
Designed by Jim Morgan

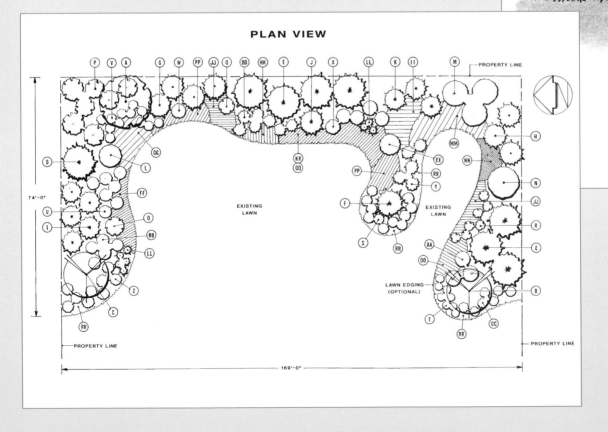

PLAN VIEW

Regional Plant Lists

Because climate and growing conditions vary greatly throughout North America, it is impossible to list here specific plants for this landscape plan that would thrive in all regions of the country. However, you can order a Blueprint Package for this plan containing a list of plants, selected by experts, for your region.

The six-page Blueprint Package features a large-size version of this Plan View, plus a detailed Plant and Materials List. It also includes an illustrated list of hundreds of landscape plants suited to your region, to use if you wish to make substitutions, as well as planting instructions and plant adaptation maps to ensure professional-looking results.

See page 157 to order your regionalized Blueprint Package.

Evergreen and deciduous shrubs and small trees, mixed with drifts of bulbs and flowering perennials, create an ever-changing border that's gorgeous every month of the year.

Easy-Care Shrub Border

NOTHING BEATS SHRUBS AND TREES for an easy-care show of flowers and foliage throughout the year. This lovely garden includes shrubs that bloom at various times—from late winter into autumn. In autumn, the deciduous shrubs turn flaming shades of yellow, gold, orange, and red. (These colors appear even more brilliant against the deep greens of the evergreen shrubs.) During the winter, when flowers and fall foliage are finished, many plants feature glossy berries or evergreen leaves that turn deep burgundy.

A tall evergreen and two flowering trees anchor the border's widest points and balance the garden. Most shrubs are grouped in all-of-a-kind drifts to create impact, but several specimens appear alone as eye-catching focal points. A few large drifts of long-blooming perennials, interplanted with spring bulbs, break up the shrubs to give a variety of textures and forms.

Designed for the back of an average-sized lot, this border can be located in any sunny area. It makes a perfect addition to an existing property with only a high-maintenance lawn and little other landscaping, because the design adds year-round interest, creates privacy, and reduces maintenance.

LANDSCAPE PLAN L308 SHOWN IN SPRING
DESIGNED BY SALVATORE A. MASULLO

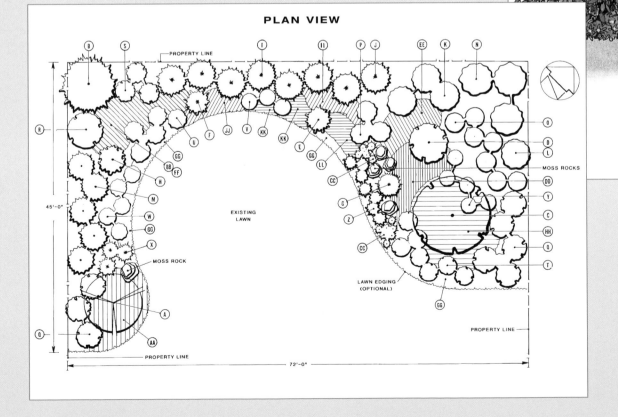

PLAN VIEW

PROPERTY LINE

EXISTING LAWN

MOSS ROCK

MOSS ROCKS

LAWN EDGING (OPTIONAL)

PROPERTY LINE

PROPERTY LINE

45'-0"

72'-0"

Regional Plant Lists

Because climate and growing conditions vary greatly throughout North America, it is impossible to list here specific plants for this landscape plan that would thrive in all regions of the country. However, you can order a Blueprint Package for this plan containing a list of plants, selected by experts, for your region.

The six-page Blueprint Package features a large-size version of this Plan View, plus a detailed Plant and Materials List. It also includes an illustrated list of hundreds of landscape plants suited to your region, to use if you wish to make substitutions, as well as planting instructions and plant adaptation maps to ensure professional-looking results.

See page 157 to order your regionalized Blueprint Package.

When easy-care, disease- and insect-resistant shrubs are used to create a border and allowed to grow naturally without excessive pruning, the result is a beautiful and practically maintenance-free garden.

Low-Maintenance Island Bed

ONE OF THE GREAT JOYS of a lovely low-maintenance garden is having the time to really enjoy it. If you'd like a garden bed that is eye-catching as well as easy-care, this design is for you. This bow-tie-shaped bed contains a delightful variety of low-maintenance perennials, evergreens, deciduous trees and shrubs, and spring bulbs. Such a diverse blend of easy-care plants guarantees you'll have both year-round color and the time to take pleasure in every season's display.

The berms at each end of the bed create a small valley that is traversed by a natural stone path. Trees screen the peak of the higher berm, adding a bit of mystery and encouraging visitors to explore. Two pathways—one of mulch, the other of stepping-stones— make it easy to enjoy the plantings up close and to perform maintenance tasks, such as occasional deadheading and weeding. Moss rocks in three areas of the garden, and a birdhouse near the stepping-stone path, provide pleasing structure and interest.

LANDSCAPE PLAN L323 SHOWN IN SUMMER
DESIGNED BY JEFFREY DIEFENBACH

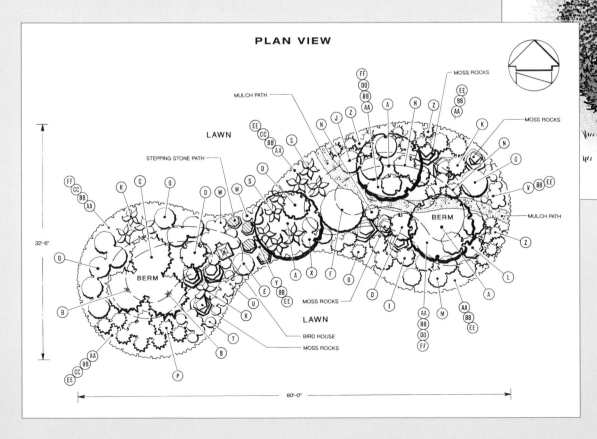

PLAN VIEW

Regional Plant Lists

Because climate and growing conditions vary greatly throughout North America, it is impossible to list here specific plants for this landscape plan that would thrive in all regions of the country. However, you can order a Blueprint Package for this plan containing a list of plants, selected by experts, for your region.

The six-page Blueprint Package features a large-size version of this Plan View, plus a detailed Plant and Materials List. It also includes an illustrated list of hundreds of landscape plants suited to your region, to use if you wish to make substitutions, as well as planting instructions and plant adaptation maps to ensure professional-looking results.

See page 157 to order your regionalized Blueprint Package.

Locate this easy-care bed in an open area of lawn in the front- or backyard to create a pretty view that can be enjoyed from both indoors and out.

Design: Tom Pellett

CHAPTER 7

SOLUTIONS FOR SHADY SITES

*Shade gardens, like those in full sun,
offer many opportunities—
and some challenges.
You'll have the chance
to grow some beautiful and colorful
shade-loving plants that
full-sun gardens can't support—
and there's an amazing number of them.
What's more, you can add
certain sun-loving plants to
lightly shaded or partly shaded gardens
if you choose wisely.
Best of all, a shady garden offers
a cool retreat during the heat of summer.*

Designed with a graceful curve, this shady border brims with flowers in spring because it features shade-loving woodland wildflowers. The high-pruned trees cast dappled shade that helps these beauties to thrive.

TYPES OF SHADE

There are basically four types of shade to consider when designing a garden:

Deep or Full Shade: All-day shade without any direct sun. This is the most difficult type of shade to work with, especially if the soil is dry because of shallow-rooted trees. You may need to water more frequently to keep plants healthy.

Part Shade: Shade for part of the day and in direct sun during the remainder. Conditions may be tricky, because many shade plants wilt if they are in shade in the morning and in full sun in the afternoon; shade plants do better with morning sun and afternoon shade. Some sun-loving plants perform well in part shade.

Light Shade: Dappled or filtered light created by high-canopied trees. The soil may be damp or dry, depending on the type of trees. Many plants grow well in light shade.

Open Shade: Often occurs in city gardens or on the north side of suburban homes, where no direct sun falls, although light and heat may be reflected from surrounding walls. The soil may be damp or dry.

Designed to play up the contrasts in foliage and flower texture and color, this border of ferns, rhododendrons, and azaleas thrives in light shade.

GARDEN COLOR IN THE SHADE

The light in shaded gardens often has a cool, bluish or greenish cast that affects the colors of the plants growing there. Too many blue and purple flowers in a shade garden can be a bit gloomy, because these colors tend to deepen and enhance shadows. White and pink look wonderful in the recesses of a shady garden, adding a bright note that livens up the design. Likewise, gold, yellow, and chartreuse add touches of sunny warmth that counteract the coolness of the shadows.

For foliar interest in tones of pink, white, and green in a shady garden, try adding some variegated foliage plants, such as 'Burgundy Glow' bugleweed, coleus, polka-dot plant, caladium, or Japanese painted fern. When designing a garden with variegated foliage, be sure to use plenty of quiet greens or blue-greens to provide a calming foil for the busy patterns of multicolored plants. For floral shades of pink and white, consider goat's beard, astilbe, azalea, foamflower, and impatiens.

For sun-kissed tones, try mixing the yellows and golds of flowering and foliage plants. For flowers, choose St.-John's-wort, marsh marigold, daffodil, 'Sulphureum' bishop's-hat, English primrose, pansy, yellow flag iris, lemon daylily, 'Golden Splendor' lily, and foxglove. For bright leaves, choose coleus; golden creeping Jenny; 'Gold Edger', 'Gold Standard', and 'Golden Tiara' hosta; 'Golden Queen' and 'Golden King' English holly; and 'Goldmound' spirea.

For chartreuse touches, use the vibrant flowers of lady's mantle to echo the edges of 'Aureo-marginata' hosta. Or combine the brilliant flowers of cushion spurge with the delicate yellowish green of full-moon maple leaves.

Design: Conni Cross

One particularly effective color scheme for a shade garden is white, which includes white- and cream-variegated foliage, such as hostas and pulmonarias, and white- and cream-colored flowers, such as impatiens, astilbe, goat's beard, and snakeroot. Or plant a pink garden with pink-variegated foliage and pink flowers, using impatiens, astilbe, 'Rubrum' lily, polka-dot plant, caladium, and coleus. A more subtle and sophisticated theme is a green garden that emphasizes the various colors and textures of foliage. For this type of garden, combine hostas, ferns, and glossy-leaved broadleaf evergreen shrubs.

TEXTURES IN THE SHADE

In deep shade, you may have to depend on foliage color and texture for interest, since the number of flowering plants that grow well under these conditions is limited. You can create all sorts of subtle, sophisticated designs using drifts of foliage plants in varying textures, from bold to delicate. You can also enhance textural contrasts by choosing neighboring plants with contrasting foliage color and by repeating a color farther away.

For example, the immense, glossy chartreuse to gold leaves of 'Sum & Substance' hosta can be used to repeat the color of the fine-textured but equally bright leaves of 'Limemound' and 'Goldmound' spirea. Plant a green hosta, such as *Hosta lancifolia*, and a green fern, such as cinnamon fern, between these plants to emphasize the differing colors and textures.

The plans in this chapter offer an array of solutions for beautifying a shady part of your yard. The designers chose the best and most beautiful shade-loving plants to carry out the designs to guarantee your success. ❧

PLANTS FOR SHADE

Annuals & Tender Bulbs

begonia *(Begonia sempervirens)*
caladium *(Caladium* x *hortulanum)*
clivia *(Clivia miniata)* *
coleus *(Coleus* x *hybridus)*
edging lobelia *(Lobelia erinus)*
impatiens *(Impatiens wallerana)*
sweet alyssum *(Lobularia maritima)*

Groundcovers

bishop's-hat *(Epimedium sulphureum)*
English ivy *(Hedera helix)* *+
foamflower *(Tiarella cordifolia)*
lily-of-the-valley *(Convallaria majalis)*
myrtle/periwinkle *(Vinca minor)* *+
sweet woodruff *(Galium odoratum)* *

Shrubs

azalea *(Rhododendron* spp.*)*
Japanese andromeda *(Pieris japonica)*
mountain laurel *(Kalmia latifolia)*
rhododendron *(Rhododendron* spp.*)*
sweet box *(Sarcococca hookerana* var. *humilis)* *+
yew *(Taxus* spp.*)* *+

Perennials & Hardy Bulbs

astilbe *(Astilbe* x *arendsii)*
bleeding heart *(Dicentra spectabilis)*
columbine *(Aquilegia canadensis)*
dead nettle *(Lamium maculatum)* +
fern (various genera and species) *
forget-me-not *(Myosotis sylvatica)*
foxglove *(Digitalis purpurea)*
goat's beard *(Aruncus dioicus)*
hosta *(Hosta* species and cultivars) *
Japanese anemone *(Anemone* x *hybrida)*
lady's mantle *(Alchemilla mollis)*
Lenten rose *(Helleborus orientalis)*
lily *(Lilium* spp.*)*
primrose *(Primula* spp.*)*
Solomon's seal *(Polygonatum odoratum)* *
sweet violet *(Viola odorata)*

*   tolerates deep shade
+   tolerates dry shade

SHADY FLOWER BORDER

If you're constantly complaining that nothing will grow in the shade of the trees in your backyard, consider planting this beautiful shady flower border. Lawn grass needs full sun and struggles to grow under trees, so why not plant something that flourishes in the shade and looks much prettier! This charming flower border features shade-loving perennials and ferns, fits under existing trees, and blooms from spring through fall.

In this design, flowering perennials grow through a low evergreen groundcover, which keeps the garden pretty even in winter, when the perennials are dormant. Also providing year-round interest are rocks and boulders, as well as a bench that invites you to sit and enjoy the pretty scene.

The designer shows this garden against a fence along the property border, but you could plant it in front of a hedge or other shrubbery and place it anywhere in your yard. If your property is smaller, you can easily eliminate the corner containing the bench and end the border with the group of three rocks to the left of the bench.

LANDSCAPE PLAN L277 SHOWN IN SUMMER
DESIGNED BY MICHAEL J. OPISSO

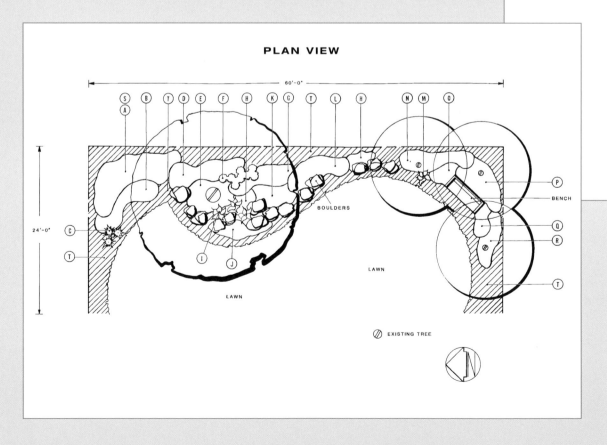

PLAN VIEW

60'-0"

24'-0"

BOULDERS

BENCH

LAWN

LAWN

⊘ EXISTING TREE

Regional Plant Lists

Because climate and growing conditions vary greatly throughout North America, it is impossible to list here specific plants for this landscape plan that would thrive in all regions of the country. However, you can order a Blueprint Package for this plan containing a list of plants, selected by experts, for your region.

The six-page Blueprint Package features a large-size version of this Plan View, plus a detailed Plant and Materials List. It also includes an illustrated list of hundreds of landscape plants suited to your region, to use if you wish to make substitutions, as well as planting instructions and plant adaptation maps to ensure professional-looking results.

See page 157 to order your regionalized Blueprint Package.

This garden of shade-loving plants flourishes under trees, where grass struggles to survive. Be sure to keep the plants healthy by providing plenty of water and fertilizer, especially if they compete for moisture and nutrients with thirsty tree roots. Thin out selected tree branches if the shade they cast is very dense.

Colorful Foliage Border

A SHADE GARDEN NEED NOT DEPEND ON FLOWERS—which usually need some sun to perform well—for color. You can enliven a shady area with a border that relies on a rainbow of foliage color to provide subtle, yet engaging beauty. An assortment of plants with variegated or unusually tinted foliage, such as burgundy, blue-green, golden yellow, and chartreuse, thrives in shady conditions. This design contains an artful mix of foliage plants with colors and textures that range from understated to bold.

In this gently curving border, the designer combines a variety of deciduous and evergreen shrubs and trees with perennials to provide year-round foliage color. Many of the plants also add floral accents to the design. The simple green of some of the evergreen plants acts as a foil for variegated and colored leaves in the border and helps to create a harmonious scene. A semicircular flagstone path leads to a bench, enticing visitors to sit in the cool shade and enjoy the splendor of the leafy display.

LANDSCAPE PLAN L324 SHOWN IN SPRING
DESIGNED BY MICHAEL J. OPISSO AND ANNE RODE

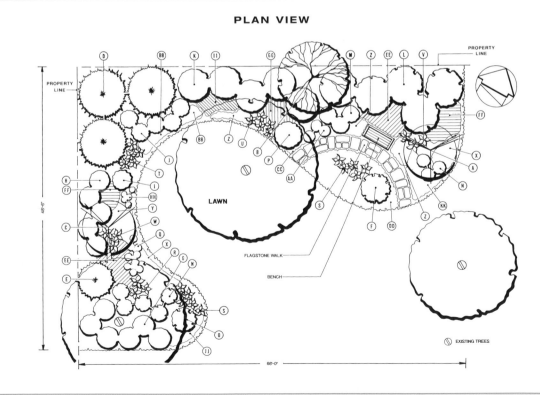

PLAN VIEW

LAWN

FLAGSTONE WALK

BENCH

PROPERTY LINE

PROPERTY LINE

EXISTING TREES

Regional Plant Lists

Because climate and growing conditions vary greatly throughout
North America, it is impossible to list here specific plants for this
landscape plan that would thrive in all regions of the country.
However, you can order a Blueprint Package for this plan containing
a list of plants, selected by experts, for your region.

The six-page Blueprint Package features a large-size version of this
Plan View, plus a detailed Plant and Materials List. It also includes an
illustrated list of hundreds of landscape plants suited to your region,
to use if you wish to make substitutions, as well as planting instructions
and plant adaptation maps to ensure professional-looking results.

See page 157 to order your regionalized Blueprint Package.

*Designed for a location where sunlight
is insufficient to support most free-
flowering plants, this showy border
derives its color from an array of shade-
loving shrubs and perennials featuring
variegated, golden or purplish red leaves.*

A shady front- or backyard can be transformed into a lovely garden setting by planting this undulating border beneath the existing trees. Modify the plan to suit the locations of your existing trees and dig planting holes for shrubs only where you will not sever tree roots that are thicker than 1 inch in diameter.

Regional Plant Lists

Because climate and growing conditions vary greatly throughout North America, it is impossible to list here specific plants for this landscape plan that would thrive in all regions of the country. However, you can order a Blueprint Package for this plan containing a list of plants, selected by experts, for your region.

The six-page Blueprint Package features a large-size version of this Plan View, plus a detailed Plant and Materials List. It also includes an illustrated list of hundreds of landscape plants suited to your region, to use if you wish to make substitutions, as well as planting instructions and plant adaptation maps to ensure professional-looking results.

See page 157 to order your regionalized Blueprint Package.

SHADE-LOVING SHRUB GARDEN

THE ROUGHLY C-SHAPED DESIGN OF THIS SHADY BED creates an eye-pleasing curve. The garden's undulating interior edge forms all kinds of interesting nooks and crannies, which invite visitors to explore. Site this bed under the spread of high-canopied trees, which offer filtered shade—the kind that allows many types of shade-loving plants to flourish.

Shade-loving shrubs dominate the bed, with drifts of spring-flowering bulbs, colonies of ferns, and groups of perennials interspersed throughout to add more color. Bulbs dot the mulched areas between the shrubs in spring. Once the bulbs finish their display and go dormant, the mulch serves as pathways into the rest of the bed.

Many of the shrubs have lovely flowers during spring and summer, followed by showy berries that appear in fall and persist through winter. The designer adds a birdbath to accommodate the birds attracted by the berry-producing shrubs. Other structural elements include a garden sculpture and a lawn path that leads to a rustic bench, where visitors can sit and enjoy the naturalistic setting.

LANDSCAPE PLAN L325 SHOWN IN SPRING
DESIGNED BY MARIA MORRISON

PLAN VIEW

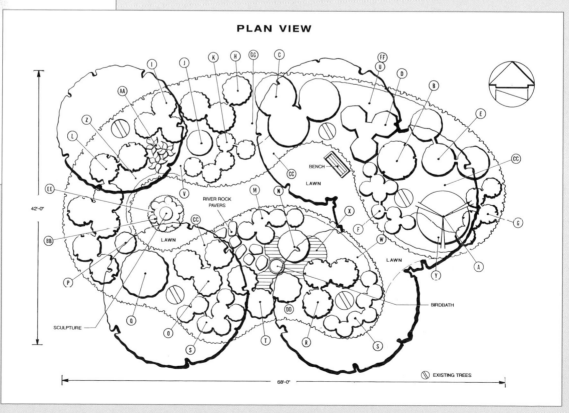

SCULPTURE

BENCH

LAWN

RIVER ROCK PAVERS

LAWN

LAWN

BIRDBATH

42'-0"

68'-0"

EXISTING TREES

Fern & Flower Glen

This naturalistic garden bed is meant to beautify an area where mature tall trees cast light shade. The designer plants several small spring-flowering trees under these existing taller trees—singly and in clusters—to create the realistic effect of a woodland, where low understory trees readily grow beneath towering deep-rooted trees. The designer places clusters of shade-loving flowering shrubs under the trees, and carpets the ground with feathery ferns, flowering perennials, and colorful foliage plants.

Two mulched paths lead through the garden, allowing you to stroll beneath the branches and sit in the shade to enjoy the scene. Several tall, narrow evergreens create a privacy screen behind the bench and direct your view inward.

This design is easily adapted to sites where existing trees don't conform exactly to the pattern shown here. Simply space the flowering trees a reasonable distance from the mature trees, adapt the placement of other plants accordingly, and give the paths a different course, if need be. The secret to the garden's success is in choosing adaptable shade-loving plants and arranging them in pretty drifts.

LANDSCAPE PLAN L326 SHOWN IN SPRING
DESIGNED BY JIM MORGAN

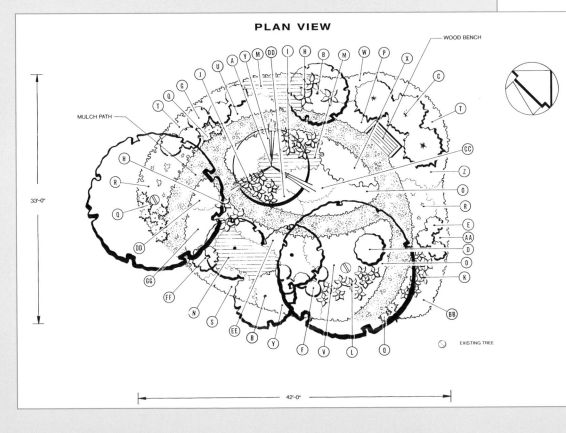

PLAN VIEW

WOOD BENCH

MULCH PATH

EXISTING TREE

33'-0"

42'-0"

Regional Plant Lists

Because climate and growing conditions vary greatly throughout North America, it is impossible to list here specific plants for this landscape plan that would thrive in all regions of the country. However, you can order a Blueprint Package for this plan containing a list of plants, selected by experts, for your region.

The six-page Blueprint Package features a large-size version of this Plan View, plus a detailed Plant and Materials List. It also includes an illustrated list of hundreds of landscape plants suited to your region, to use if you wish to make substitutions, as well as planting instructions and plant adaptation maps to ensure professional-looking results.

See page 157 to order your regionalized Blueprint Package.

Instead of struggling to grow a lawn in a shady site, try planting this charming flower- and fern-filled bed to dress up the area. The plants used here will flourish under deep-rooted, high-branched trees.

Plant this lovely pond garden where its shade-loving plants will flourish. You'll enjoy the beauty of this design all year long.

Regional Plant Lists

Because climate and growing conditions vary greatly throughout North America, it is impossible to list here specific plants for this landscape plan that would thrive in all regions of the country. However, you can order a Blueprint Package for this plan containing a list of plants, selected by experts, for your region.

The six-page Blueprint Package features a large-size version of this Plan View, plus a detailed Plant and Materials List. It also includes an illustrated list of hundreds of landscape plants suited to your region, to use if you wish to make substitutions, as well as planting instructions and plant adaptation maps to ensure professional-looking results.

See page 157 to order your regionalized Blueprint Package.

SHADY POND GARDEN

DESIGNED TO BE AN OASIS IN THE SHADE, these garden beds surround a dramatic, yet naturalistic focal point: a small pond. The three lobes of the centrally located pond dictate the rhythm and design concept of the surrounding beds. Visitors enter the garden via one of three entrances, which divide it into three distinct beds—a large semicircular bed to the northwest, a roughly S-shaped bed to the southwest, and an island bed in the center, nearest the pond. Stepping-stones, set on a slightly sunken ridge, cut across the pond and allow visitors a panoramic view of the garden from the central stone.

Mid-sized evergreens ring the entire garden, giving it a sense of privacy and seclusion. A diverse mix of shade-loving flowering shrubs and trees, ferns, and perennials provides varying texture and color throughout the year.

Site this garden under existing high-canopied trees. To prevent fallen tree leaves from clogging the pond and fouling the water, cover the pond surface in autumn with bird netting. The black netting is almost invisible and allows you to easily catch and scoop out the leaves.

LANDSCAPE PLAN L327 SHOWN IN SPRING
DESIGNED BY SALVATORE A. MASULLO

PLAN VIEW

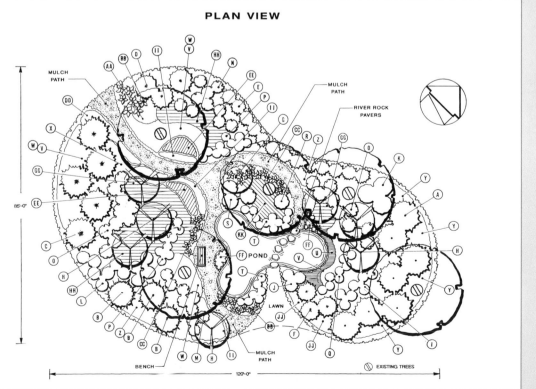

Chapter 8

Gardens for Nature Lovers

*Designed to look as if Mother Nature
arranged the plants, rocks, and
water features, a naturalistic garden—
even if it's only a small one—
brings the peaceful feeling
and sounds of the wilderness to your yard.
It's a quiet and serene garden
punctuated by the music of
singing birds and bubbling water
from a naturalistic stream or waterfall.
Other natural elements,
such as mossy rocks and weathered logs,
further enhance the wild setting
you're trying to create.*

*Even though it's designed to resemble a natural meadow, this garden
employs a few tricks to enhance its beauty. Flowers are massed in
places to create impact, and the wood-chip path curves out of sight to
draw visitors into the garden.*

PLANTS IN THE NATURALISTIC GARDEN

Whether your naturalistic bed or border is planted with native plants or exotics, what's important is how they are arranged—not in stiff rows but in a slightly haphazard fashion, as if they sprang up there naturally. This effect can be difficult to achieve without looking messy or contrived. You'll be more successful if you study how plants grow in nature. For example, if you observe plants growing in an undisturbed woodland, meadow, or rocky outcropping, you will notice the following:

- Plants grow in layers. Taller trees shelter lower shrubs, which in turn shelter low-growing wildflowers, ferns, and groundcovers.

- Many plants grow in clusters. Some types of plants—both shrubs and flowers—have creeping roots and spread to form large stands or groups.

- Some plants grow singly. Certain types of plants spread by seed and are naturally isolated from each other, rarely forming dense stands of one-of-a-kind plants.

- Some plants grow best in the shelter of a rock, tree trunk, or log. They start at the base of the rock or other object, then spread outward.

Garden designers learn lessons from these observations. They arrange some plants in wide, ground-covering drifts and then

This garden pool resembles a real pond, with rocks and boulders carefully placed near its edge so that they overhang the water or emerge from the ground in a natural way.

Design: Conni Cross

scatter individual plants throughout these drifts. They locate the rootball of ground-covering plants at the base of a boulder or other object in the garden, allowing the top growth to spread out gracefully. And they arrange the entire planting in layers. For instance, a naturalistic border might resemble a small woodland, with groups of flowering shrubs layered beneath small flowering trees; large swaths of wildflowers and groundcovers carpeting the soil; and ferns springing up here and there among taller plants.

Attract birds to your garden by landscaping with shrubs and trees that produce the types of berries and seeds birds find appetizing. These cranberrybush viburnum berries ripen in fall, when migrating birds stock up on food.

WATER IN THE NATURALISTIC GARDEN

Nothing is more natural than water in a garden. A water feature can enhance a naturalistic garden as long as it is designed to look like a real pond or stream. You can do this by giving the feature an organic shape, not a straight-sided one, and enhancing its edges with stones and rocks. You might even wish to place a large boulder so it bursts through the water's surface.

By using a flexible liner rather than a fiberglass form to build the pond, you can achieve a more realistic shape that will best fit the contours of your property. Use a liner to create a waterfall and cover up the plastic with smooth stones and rocks to give it a realistic appearance and create babbling sounds. Allow the water to flow over several cascades made from flat, rocky outcroppings and small boulders. This creates enchanting sound effects, too. The recirculating pump that powers the waterfall and stream should be hidden behind rocks so that you will not see or hear it.

BIRDS IN THE NATURALISTIC GARDEN

One of the best things about a naturalistic garden is that it often attracts wildlife, especially songbirds. Birds will flock to your garden and become permanent inhabitants if you provide them with ample food, water, shelter, and nesting sites. The easiest and most natural way to supply food is to grow plants that bear seeds and fruits that birds

can eat. If you like, you can also set out bird feeders filled with seeds to augment the natural supply.

Birds tend to visit a garden that offers a shallow source of water even if there isn't much food around. A naturalistic pond, fountain, or stream not only enhances the realism of your garden, but also attracts birds if there are shallow areas where they can drink and bathe. Although a birdbath is not technically naturalistic, it has a place in a wildlife garden as a focal point and wildlife attraction, so don't hesitate to add one if a pond is not in your budget. Some birds also like to indulge in dust baths, so you may want to set aside an open area of dry soil or grit for this purpose.

Birdhouses designed to attract particular types of birds make eye-catching focal points in a garden and may attract the birds you seek. However, dense shrubbery and evergreen trees provide the most natural nesting locations and do an excellent job of sheltering birds from the elements.

The five garden designs presented in this chapter will delight any nature lover. They'll draw songbirds to your yard and create a serene setting that's yours to enjoy. ❧

SONGBIRD BORDER

THIS ATTRACTIVE BORDER does double duty, because it serves both as a beautiful landscape planting as well as an effective wildlife sanctuary. Offering natural food sources, shelter, and water, the planting brings birds to your property throughout the year, while its informal but tidy design looks right at home in any suburban setting. Although they serve a practical purpose as well, the birdhouses, bird feeders, and birdbath add interesting architectural elements to the design

The shrubs and trees used in the border—and even many of the perennials and ornamental grasses—produce berries and seeds that attract birds. They are arranged informally and should be left unpruned to form a dense shelter for nesting sites. Because most berried plants produce best when cross-pollinated by another similar plant, the designer masses specimens together and repeats plants.

You can site this border along the property lines in either your front- or backyard, or round off its corners and use it as an island planting. Then sit back and enjoy the birds and birdsong that fill your garden.

LANDSCAPE PLAN L328 SHOWN IN AUTUMN
DESIGNED BY SALVATORE A. MASULLO

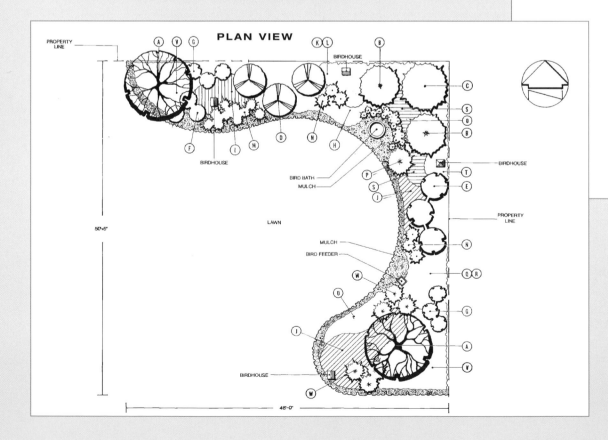

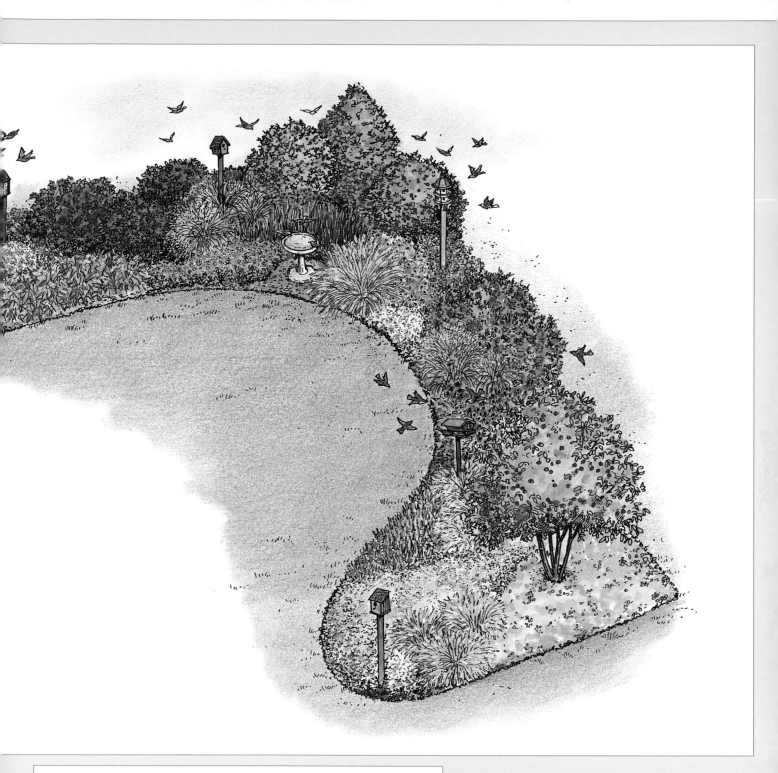

Regional Plant Lists

Because climate and growing conditions vary greatly throughout North America, it is impossible to list here specific plants for this landscape plan that would thrive in all regions of the country. However, you can order a Blueprint Package for this plan containing a list of plants, selected by experts, for your region.

The six-page Blueprint Package features a large-size version of this Plan View, plus a detailed Plant and Materials List. It also includes an illustrated list of hundreds of landscape plants suited to your region, to use if you wish to make substitutions, as well as planting instructions and plant adaptation maps to ensure professional-looking results.

See page 157 to order your regionalized Blueprint Package.

Filled with fruiting shrubs, trees, ornamental grasses, and perennials that provide food for birds, this border is as beautiful as it is bird-friendly.

WATERFALL GARDEN

MIMICKING THE WAY WATER FLOWS IN NATURE, the waterfall in this double garden pond cascades in a sheet from a small high pool to a lower larger one. To increase the natural appearance of the ponds, the designer includes several rocks to peak above water level in the lower pool. The rocks also act as natural perches for the birds, frogs, and turtles that are attracted to the water.

Echoing the cascading waterfall, many of the plants used in the design have flowing, weeping forms. Three tall flowering trees anchor the design with a drapery of branches. The arching branches of a shrubby tree soften the rocky edge of the pond with foliage. Beneath the trees, an assortment of shrubs, perennials, and groundcovers provides a changing color display from spring through autumn.

The bed is planted on a small berm, which provides the height needed for the waterfall. Stone steps climb the back of the berm and lead into the path and sitting area, which are made from naturalistic irregular flagstones. The ponds are easily constructed with a flexible liner that is concealed by rocks and stones.

LANDSCAPE PLAN L329 SHOWN IN SPRING
DESIGNED BY FRANK L. ESPOSITO

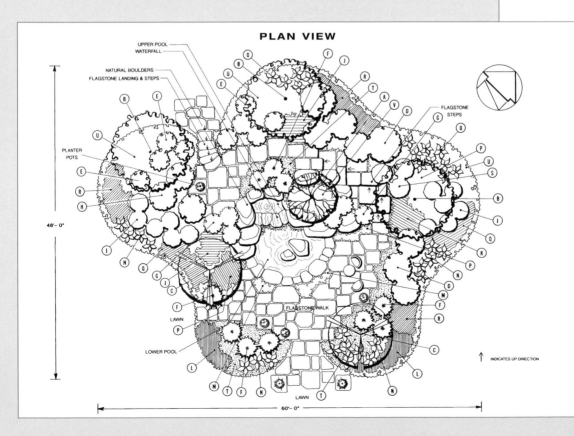

PLAN VIEW

UPPER POOL
WATERFALL

NATURAL BOULDERS
FLAGSTONE LANDING & STEPS

FLAGSTONE STEPS

PLANTER POTS

48'– 0"

FLAGSTONE WALK

LAWN

LOWER POOL

LAWN

INDICATES UP DIRECTION

60'– 0"

Regional Plant Lists

Because climate and growing conditions vary greatly throughout North America, it is impossible to list here specific plants for this landscape plan that would thrive in all regions of the country. However, you can order a Blueprint Package for this plan containing a list of plants, selected by experts, for your region.

The six-page Blueprint Package features a large-size version of this Plan View, plus a detailed Plant and Materials List. It also includes an illustrated list of hundreds of landscape plants suited to your region, to use if you wish to make substitutions, as well as planting instructions and plant adaptation maps to ensure professional-looking results.

See page 157 to order your regionalized Blueprint Package.

Bring the feeling of the great outdoors to your backyard with this garden pond and waterfall. The scenery is filled with rugged stones and soft flowers and foliage—a perfect naturalistic getaway.

BIRD-FRIENDLY SHRUB BORDER

THIS BORDER INCLUDES EVERYTHING BIRDS NEED—food, water, and nesting sites—and encourages them to become permanent residents of your yard. The design curves inward, creating a sense of enclosure and a sanctuary that appeals to even the shiest types of birds. The border's attractive design includes a pond, birdhouse, and birdbath, which act as focal points and make the garden irresistible to people as well.

The large variety of pretty fruiting shrubs offers birds natural nourishment throughout much of the year, but you can supplement the food supply with store-bought bird food if you wish. Deciduous and evergreen trees provide shelter and nesting places, while the mulched areas give birds a place to take dust baths and to poke around for insects and worms.

Because water is so important to birds, the garden includes two water features: a small naturalistic pond, and a birdbath set in a circular bed. Both offer spots for perching, bathing, and drinking. In cold-weather climates, consider adding a special heater to the birdbath to keep the water from freezing; water attracts birds in winter even more than birdseed.

LANDSCAPE PLAN L330 SHOWN IN SUMMER
DESIGNED BY MICHAEL J. OPISSO

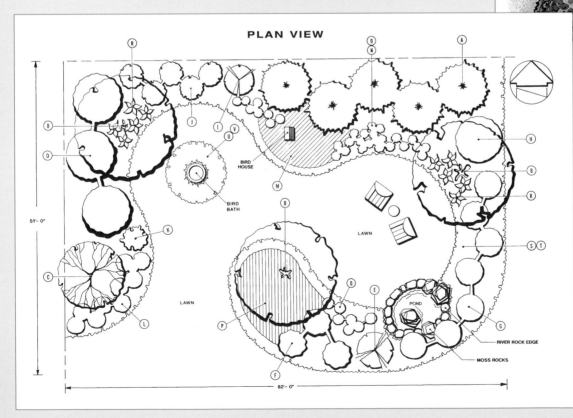

PLAN VIEW

BIRD HOUSE

BIRD BATH

LAWN

LAWN

POND

RIVER ROCK EDGE

MOSS ROCKS

5T'- 0"

82'- 0"

Regional Plant Lists

Because climate and growing conditions vary greatly throughout North America, it is impossible to list here specific plants for this landscape plan that would thrive in all regions of the country. However, you can order a Blueprint Package for this plan containing a list of plants, selected by experts, for your region.

The six-page Blueprint Package features a large-size version of this Plan View, plus a detailed Plant and Materials List. It also includes an illustrated list of hundreds of landscape plants suited to your region, to use if you wish to make substitutions, as well as planting instructions and plant adaptation maps to ensure professional-looking results.

See page 157 to order your regionalized Blueprint Package.

Birds flock to this border, which provides them with ample supplies of food and water and locations for nesting, and bathing. There's plenty of room for bird-watchers as well.

Sit beneath the flower-draped pergola and enjoy glimpses of hummingbirds as they pause in midflight to drink nectar and splash in the birdbath.

Regional Plant Lists

Because climate and growing conditions vary greatly throughout North America, it is impossible to list here specific plants for this landscape plan that would thrive in all regions of the country. However, you can order a Blueprint Package for this plan containing a list of plants, selected by experts, for your region.

The six-page Blueprint Package features a large-size version of this Plan View, plus a detailed Plant and Materials List. It also includes an illustrated list of hundreds of landscape plants suited to your region, to use if you wish to make substitutions, as well as planting instructions and plant adaptation maps to ensure professional-looking results.

See page 157 to order your regionalized Blueprint Package.

HUMMINGBIRD BED

YOUR YARD WILL BE HOME to jewel-toned, quicksilver hummingbirds once you install this colorful bed. A rich display of bright annuals and perennials, specially selected to attract hummingbirds, creates a delightful setting. All birds need water, and hummingbirds are particularly attracted to flowing water, so the birdbath in this design features a small bubbler device.

Informal flagstone pavers lead through the garden to a semicircular mulched area set with flagstones that surround the birdbath. The path to the wooden pergola, which creates a lovely sitting area, leads through the pretty flowers. Climbing vines and hanging planters attached to the pergola provide additional nectar and create a pleasant shady area where you can watch the hummers dart by. Hang the pots so you can watch the birds at eye level from the sitting area. Neutral-colored plastic pots look best and cut down on evaporation, minimizing watering chores.

Site this design in a sunny location close to your house so you can observe the birds from indoors as well. Or, if you prefer, locate the bed in a quiet corner of your yard to enhance the tranquil atmosphere.

LANDSCAPE PLAN L331 SHOWN IN SUMMER
DESIGNED BY PATRICK J. DUFFE

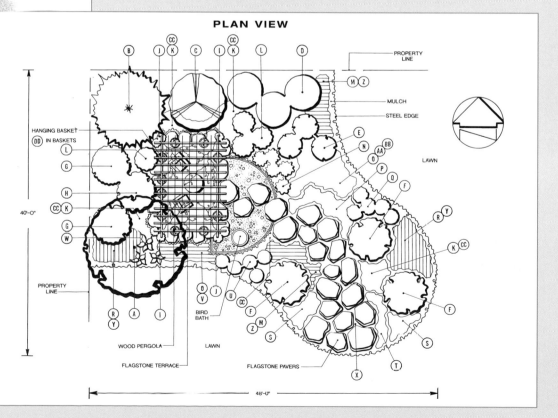

PLAN VIEW

A gently curving patio area, set in the middle of this naturalistic planting, is the perfect place for a comfortable bench or table and chairs.

Regional Plant Lists

Because climate and growing conditions vary greatly throughout North America, it is impossible to list here specific plants for this landscape plan that would thrive in all regions of the country. However, you can order a Blueprint Package for this plan containing a list of plants, selected by experts, for your region.

The six-page Blueprint Package features a large-size version of this Plan View, plus a detailed Plant and Materials List. It also includes an illustrated list of hundreds of landscape plants suited to your region, to use if you wish to make substitutions, as well as planting instructions and plant adaptation maps to ensure professional-looking results.

See page 157 to order your regionalized Blueprint Package.

NATURALISTIC POND PLANTING

A SMALL, SERENE POND serves as the centerpiece of this informal garden bed, enticing visitors to come and sit a spell. The irregular flagstones and natural river rocks around the pond's edge form a semicircular patio area that makes a perfect spot for contemplating the plantings, relaxing, or bird-watching. If you'd like to include the sound of falling water in the scene, consider adding a small bubbler-type fountain to the pond.

The design's simple, curving geometry and informal style make it suitable for either a front yard or backyard. Because the far side of the planting features tall evergreens and flowering trees, the bed could be easily turned into a privacy planting and used as the border of a small property. Or it could be situated in an open area of a larger property to create an intimate space.

Construct the pond from a flexible liner, or choose a pre-fabricated pond with a naturalistic shape. You can stock the pond with goldfish and grow waterlilies and other aquatic plants in submerged tubs, as long as the water is at least 18 inches deep.

LANDSCAPE PLAN L332 SHOWN IN SUMMER
DESIGNED BY PATRICK J. DUFFE

PLAN VIEW

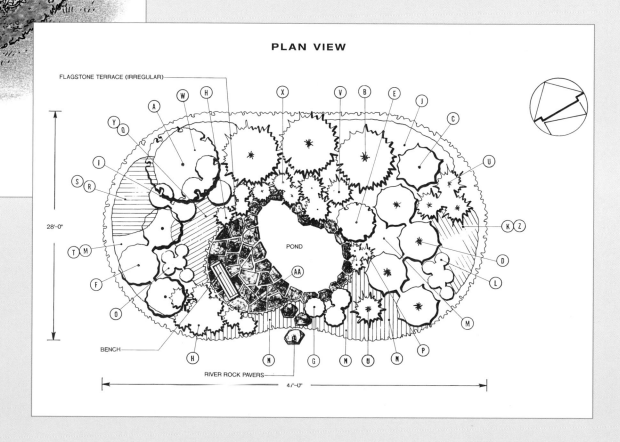

CHAPTER 9

DESIGNS FOR GARDEN RETREATS

For many people, a garden is
a quiet and peaceful place to retreat
from the cares of everyday life.
It's a place to enjoy the outdoors while
puttering among the flowers,
or a place to stretch out in the sun or shade
while reading a magazine or novel.
The five designs presented in this chapter
can help you turn a nook or corner of your yard
into a garden retreat where you can find
a cherished bit of solitude.
Each design fits nicely into the larger context
of a backyard or side yard.
All of these gardens create an atmosphere
of serenity within their boundaries,
seemingly remote from the rest of the world.

A bench set beneath a cozy rose-covered arbor in this flower-filled
border creates a romantic garden retreat, where it's possible to escape
from the world for a few minutes or even hours.

Design: Kitty Taylor

you can still create a garden retreat. The trick is to screen the garden from view with either plants, such as a hedge or tall perennials, or with hardscape elements, such as a wall, fence, or gateway, or with a combination of hardscape and softscape elements, such as a rose-covered trellis or pergola.

A successful garden retreat also creates a sense of discovery and surprise. Curving pathways and partially obscured views

An attractive bench becomes an inviting retreat when landscaped with paving stones and a pretty skirt of flowering plants around its feet.

CREATING A GARDEN RETREAT

A retreat is a private place, open to others by invitation only. It conjures romantic images of winding pathways, voluptuous flowers, and a flower-covered pergola or a gazebo where you can sit and daydream. A garden retreat might include the soothing sound of water splashing in the background. This sound is especially useful for drowning out distracting noises such as traffic or neighbors.

By definition, a retreat is secluded, quiet, and, most importantly, visually removed from other structures. Unless you live on a sprawling country estate, your home is most likely within sight of your entire yard. It's still possible to create a hidden retreat even in a small yard. In fact, a pocket-sized area, such as a narrow side yard, already has the advantage of being tucked away around the side of your house. If you have a large, open, relatively flat yard,

Flowering Vines for Creating Privacy

Vines grow quickly, draping over structures to create a romantic flowering bower that gives any garden a romantic sense of privacy. Here are some fast-growing woody vines to include in your garden retreat.

Spring-blooming
anemone clematis (*Clematis montana*)
Armand clematis (*Clematis armandii*)
Bank's rose (*Rosa banksiae*)
Carolina jessamine (*Gelsemium sempervirens*)
cross vine (*Bignonia capreolata*)
five-leaf akebia (*Akebia quinata*)
wisteria (*Wisteria* spp.)

Summer-blooming
climbing roses (*Rosa* hybrids)
Dutchman's pipe (*Aristolochia durior*)
goldflame honeysuckle (*Lonicera* x *heckrottii*)
large-flowered hybrid clematis (*Clematis* x *hybrida*)
trumpet honeysuckle (*Lonicera sempervirens*)

Late summer- and fall-blooming
silver fleecevine (*Polygonum aubertii*)
sweet autumn clematis (*Clematis maximowicziana*)
porcelain berry (*Ampelopsis brevipedunculata* 'Elegans')
trumpet creeper (*Campsis radicans*)

are classic design devices for this type of garden. You might consider installing a retreat behind a slight rise or among a stand of established trees to increase the sense of enclosure and privacy. Another particularly effective design tactic is to frame a slice of the view into a retreat with a lovely gate set into a stone wall, fence, or hedge. This provides just a glimpse into the garden, enhancing its romance.

Design: Conni Cross

Suspended from the trees in a nook in a woodland garden, this hammock offers the perfect place to relax with a good book.

A Sense of Style

A garden retreat can be as formal or as naturalistic, as large or as compact, as you like. For a formal effect, plan the bed or border around a fancy ironwork bench, or a table and chairs. You can enclose a formal retreat with a brick wall or fancy trelliswork, or with a neatly trimmed hedge. For a more rustic look, consider using natural-colored Adirondack chairs or twig furniture in your retreat. The garden furnishings, as well as the selection and layout of the plants, define the style of your garden.

If your space is very limited, a cozy hammock set in a shady corner and screened by a bit of flower-covered latticework can be just as effective as an elaborate gazebo set in a large bed. Or you may want to consider installing a flower-covered arbor above a bench. Set the bench and arbor at a small distance from a pathway or tuck them into a quiet corner of your yard; and you'll have a great getaway just moments from your back door.

Each design presented in this chapter fits nicely into a backyard or side yard and can turn any space in your yard into a quiet retreat, seemingly at a great distance from the rest of the world. You might choose the Romantic Gazebo Planting if a turn-of-the-century garden retreat is your style. Or the Secret Garden may be the answer to your landscape needs if you prefer more formality closer to the house. Whatever your preferences, one of the five designs in this chapter is sure to please you. ❧

Sit here in solitude, or with friends and family, and enjoy the sounds of splashing water and singing birds. This bed can be placed almost anywhere on your property to create a beautifully private scene.

Regional Plant Lists

Because climate and growing conditions vary greatly throughout North America, it is impossible to list here specific plants for this landscape plan that would thrive in all regions of the country. However, you can order a Blueprint Package for this plan containing a list of plants, selected by experts, for your region.

The six-page Blueprint Package features a large-size version of this Plan View, plus a detailed Plant and Materials List. It also includes an illustrated list of hundreds of landscape plants suited to your region, to use if you wish to make substitutions, as well as planting instructions and plant adaptation maps to ensure professional-looking results.

See page 157 to order your regionalized Blueprint Package.

Secluded Fountain Planting

DESIGNED TO BE A BACKYARD OASIS, this mixed garden bed features a gently curving path that leads to a secluded patio and fountain. Deciduous trees and shrubs, evergreens, ornamental grasses, and perennials blend together to create a privacy screen around the seating area. The sense of enclosure is further enhanced with a low berm behind the wall surrounding the fountain. In this intimate setting, you can sit and relax while listening to the music of the splashing fountain.

The designer edged the semicircular fountain basin with stone that matches the patio and walkway to visually unite the design.

The varied and dense plantings of this design are attracitve to wildlife. As an added bonus, this heavily planted garden leaves little room for pesky weeds to take hold. And because this is a naturalistic garden, there's no need to keep a rigid maintenance schedule. Occasional deadheading and pruning to maintain plant health are the only gardening musts.

LANDSCAPE PLAN L333 SHOWN IN SUMMER
DESIGNED BY JEFFERY DIEFFENBACH

PLAN VIEW

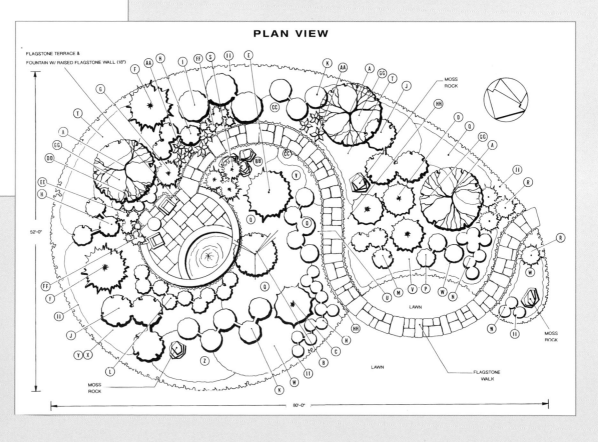

FLAGSTONE TERRACE &
FOUNTAIN W/ RAISED FLAGSTONE WALL (18")

MOSS ROCK

MOSS ROCK

52'-0"

LAWN

LAWN

MOSS ROCK

MOSS ROCK

FLAGSTONE WALK

80'-0"

Capture the romance of a bygone era with this romantic gazebo garden. The flower-filled setting creates a very special retreat that would work as the centerpiece of almost any backyard.

Regional Plant Lists

Because climate and growing conditions vary greatly throughout North America, it is impossible to list here specific plants for this landscape plan that would thrive in all regions of the country. However, you can order a Blueprint Package for this plan containing a list of plants, selected by experts, for your region.

The six-page Blueprint Package features a large-size version of this Plan View, plus a detailed Plant and Materials List. It also includes an illustrated list of hundreds of landscape plants suited to your region, to use if you wish to make substitutions, as well as planting instructions and plant adaptation maps to ensure professional-looking results.

See page 157 to order your regionalized Blueprint Package.

ROMANTIC GAZEBO PLANTING

THIS ROOMY GAZEBO FORMS the centerpiece of a beautiful garden setting, evoking the romance of a bygone era. Fragrant vines climb up the back of the structure and spread out over the roof, creating even more privacy and filling the air with their delightful perfume. Here's a special garden where you can eat by candlelight on a summer evening, or simply hide out from the world on a hot afternoon.

Three different trees give the design height, which offsets the size of the gazebo, while also offering overhead color at various times of the year. Carpeting the ground under the trees is a compatible combination of easy-care shrubs, perennials, and groundcovers. A stepping-stone path leads through the garden, with two entrances from the lawn, and circles the gazebo to make tending the garden easy.

Groups of boulders anchor the design, giving it a naturalistic feel and echoing the stones in the paths. One cluster of boulders is designed as a bubbling fountain, creating a pleasant sound that can be enjoyed by visitors to the gazebo or anyone resting on the nearby bench.

LANDSCAPE PLAN L334 SHOWN IN SUMMER
DESIGNED BY JANIS LEONTI

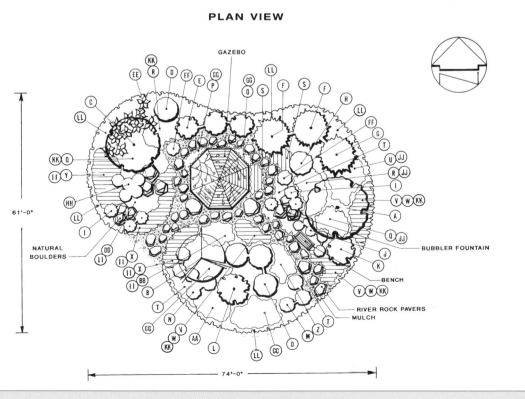

PLAN VIEW

Only invited guests enjoy the delights of this formal garden, which is designed to be hidden from public view.

Regional Plant Lists

Because climate and growing conditions vary greatly throughout North America, it is impossible to list here specific plants for this landscape plan that would thrive in all regions of the country. However, you can order a Blueprint Package for this plan containing a list of plants, selected by experts, for your region.

The six-page Blueprint Package features a large-size version of this Plan View, plus a detailed Plant and Materials List. It also includes an illustrated list of hundreds of landscape plants suited to your region, to use if you wish to make substitutions, as well as planting instructions and plant adaptation maps to ensure professional-looking results.

See page 157 to order your regionalized Blueprint Package.

SECRET GARDEN

TUCKED INTO A CORNER BY THE HOUSE, hidden from view by a high hedge, accessible only through an arbored gate or an entrance from the house, this garden is so secluded that it remains a secret from anyone in the rest of the yard. The designer keeps this secret garden essentially formal in design so that its lines and plants create a restful scene.

Three tall shade trees at the garden's corners create symmetry and further enhance the feeling of privacy. These trees and the formal hedge rest in an expanse of groundcover, which gives them a pretty skirt while also discouraging weeds. The groundcover extends under the hedge into the secret garden, dressing up the beds of flowering shrubs, bulbs, and perennials.

The flagstone walk meanders through the garden to avoid an overly formal effect. The sculpture in the center of the garden creates a focal point that can be enjoyed from anywhere in the garden, but especially when viewed from the corner bench. Plants, walk, and sculpture all combine here to create a pretty viewing garden within the hedge walls.

LANDSCAPE PLAN L335 SHOWN IN SUMMER
DESIGNED BY MICHAEL J. OPISSO

PLAN VIEW

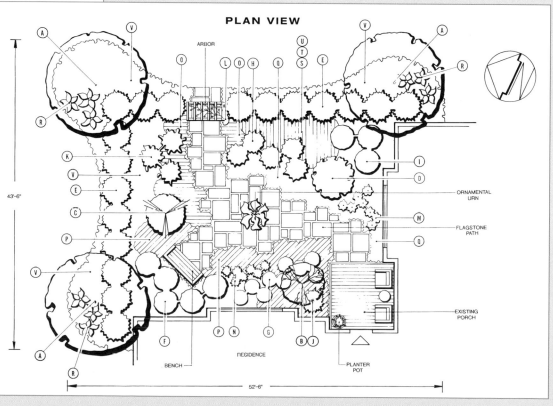

Site this beautiful pergola and its surrounding garden bed at a distance from the house, where it creates a dramatic focal point that draws visitors to come and explore.

Regional Plant Lists

Because climate and growing conditions vary greatly throughout North America, it is impossible to list here specific plants for this landscape plan that would thrive in all regions of the country. However, you can order a Blueprint Package for this plan containing a list of plants, selected by experts, for your region.

The six-page Blueprint Package features a large-size version of this Plan View, plus a detailed Plant and Materials List. It also includes an illustrated list of hundreds of landscape plants suited to your region, to use if you wish to make substitutions, as well as planting instructions and plant adaptation maps to ensure professional-looking results.

See page 157 to order your regionalized Blueprint Package.

Pergola Planting

SITTING IN THE OPEN SHADE CAST BY THIS PERGOLA evokes the secure feeling of being in an outdoor room—a room where you can fully enjoy the flowers in the surrounding garden. This plan's designer enhances the feeling of an outdoor room by adding lattice panels to the ends of the pergola, enclosing it further and providing the perfect place for a colorful cover of climbing vines.

Meant to be situated in an open area of the yard, this pergola planting creates a decorative centerpiece in the lawn—you can site it in either the front or backyard. To prevent the pergola from looking too massive and dominant, the designer adds several tall trees to the bed, off-setting and balancing its size and shape, and anchoring it to the surrounding landscape.

The flagstone patio under the pergola has two entrance paths from the lawn—one on each long side—so that you can walk through the garden. That way, the large island planting becomes a lovely destination rather than an obstacle in the middle of the lawn.

LANDSCAPE PLAN L336 SHOWN IN SUMMER
DESIGNED BY FRANK L. ESPOSITO

PLAN VIEW

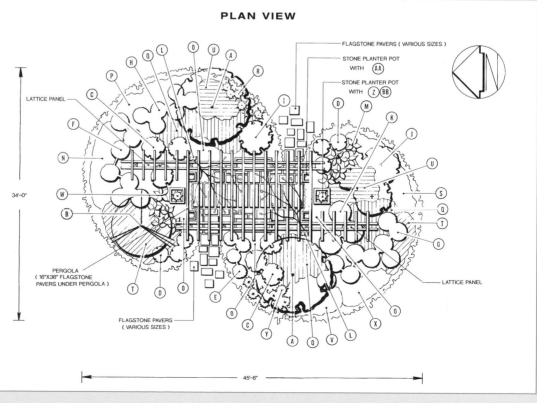

FLAGSTONE PAVERS (VARIOUS SIZES)

STONE PLANTER POT WITH (AA)

STONE PLANTER POT WITH (Z) (BB)

LATTICE PANEL

34'-0"

PERGOLA
(16"X36" FLAGSTONE
PAVERS UNDER PERGOLA)

FLAGSTONE PAVERS
(VARIOUS SIZES)

LATTICE PANEL

45'-6"

Quiet Pocket Garden

LOCATE THIS CIRCULAR BED in a large open area of your front- or backyard, where it will create a beautiful island of flowers and foliage. The garden becomes a focal point of the yard, and because it contains evergreens and small flowering trees and shrubs, it also provides privacy by blocking views into and out of the yard. Best of all, the planting is designed so you can stroll along a curving stepping-stone path into its center to discover a secluded sitting area within.

This private sitting area is formed from an open pocket in the center of the bed that features paving stones, two curved benches, and an overhead structure. These elements furnish and define the pocket, creating the atmosphere of a garden room—a secluded outdoor retreat. There you can sit in quiet solitude, if you wish, but there's also room enough for the whole family.

The garden's year-round structure comes from its trees, shrubs, stones, and pergola. During the growing season, an assortment of colorful flowering perennials and foliage plants fleshes out the scene, creating a changing show.

LANDSCAPE PLAN L337 SHOWN IN SPRING
DESIGNED BY TIMOTHY BARRY & PAUL ROEDEL

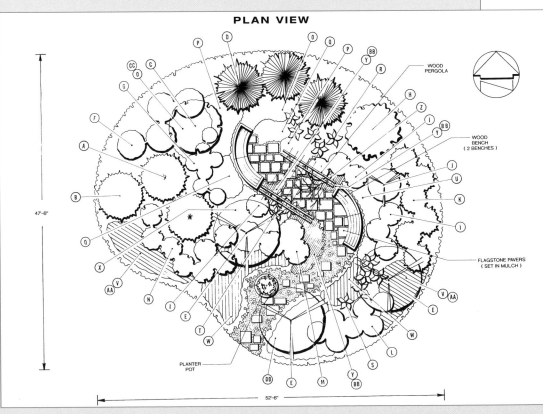

PLAN VIEW

WOOD PERGOLA

WOOD BENCH (2 BENCHES)

FLAGSTONE PAVERS (SET IN MULCH)

PLANTER POT

47'–6"

52'–6"

Regional Plant Lists

Because climate and growing conditions vary greatly throughout
North America, it is impossible to list here specific plants for this
landscape plan that would thrive in all regions of the country.
However, you can order a Blueprint Package for this plan containing
a list of plants, selected by experts, for your region.

The six-page Blueprint Package features a large-size version of this
Plan View, plus a detailed Plant and Materials List. It also includes an
illustrated list of hundreds of landscape plants suited to your region,
to use if you wish to make substitutions, as well as planting instructions
and plant adaptation maps to ensure professional-looking results.

See page 157 to order your regionalized Blueprint Package.

*The surprise in this design is an open
area situated within the center of the
bed where two dramatically curving
benches and an overhead structure
create an outdoor sitting room.*

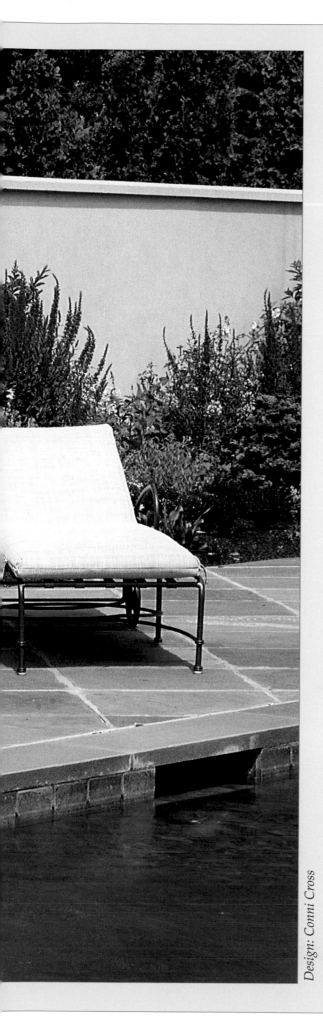

CHAPTER 10

GARDENS FOR PATIOS, DECKS & POOLSIDES

*Anyplace you spend time
sitting or entertaining outdoors
can be enhanced and made more enjoyable
with beautiful plantings.
A flower- and foliage-filled border
along a deck, patio, or pool
integrates the structure
into the surrounding landscape
and creates a pretty view.
Fragrant plants make especially
delightful additions to a sitting area—
some are so fragrant
that they perfume the air around them,
providing a natural source of aromatherapy.
Here are five designs to enhance
the outdoor areas that you use most often.*

Design: Conni Cross

The border between this pool's security wall and flagstone patio relies on vibrant summer-blooming perennials for maximum color and interest when the area is used most.

DESIGNING A DECKSIDE PLANTING

Because most decks are elevated to create a level sitting area on sloping ground, a planting ideally serves several purposes: it camouflages the deck's footings and helps blend the structure into the landscape; it frames a view from the deck without blocking the view entirely; and it brings flowers or interesting foliage up to or near eye level.

Use permanent woody plants such as dwarf evergreens and dense deciduous shrubs to camouflage the deck's footings throughout the year. Depending on the deck's height, you might wish to incorporate a few tall shrubs and small flowering trees so that they peek over the deck railing, to create a sense of enclosure and bring the flowers up to eye level. Lower plantings in the border will help camouflage the deck's footings and create a pretty scene when the deck is viewed from a distance. Carefully position a tall shade tree on the west side of the deck so that it casts shade where you want it during the hottest part of the day.

DESIGNING A PATIO PLANTING

Because a patio is usually at ground level, use lower plantings along its edges to avoid creating a closed-in feeling. Bring flowers, ornamental grasses, and low shrubs right up to its borders, but leave some areas open to the lawn. A formal planting can be softened by installing low spreading rock garden-type plants in pockets in the patio. Locate taller shrubs and evergreens near the patio, but not right next to it, to create a privacy screen that does not feel claustrophobic.

Adding Color with Containers

Containers brimming with long-blooming annuals can bring color close to your sitting area on a deck or patio and thus integrate the area with the surrounding garden. Container plantings look best if they are large in scale—24- or 36-inch pots containing a variety of plants to make a dramatic statement. Or try grouping smaller, and easier-to-move, pots in clusters of various shapes and sizes to make an effective statement. Containers need a lot of water; you

A low stone wall creates raised planting areas around this handsome brick patio, providing pleasing dimensions and highly visible plantings in this small area.

Design: Philhower Nursery

can easily keep them moist with an incon-spicuous drip-irrigation system whose lines can be concealed beneath the decking.

<u>DESIGNING A POOLSIDE PLANTING</u>
Plantings alongside a swimming pool give it a beautiful setting, and if designed right can create the illusion of a real pond if the pool's liner is a dark color. Ornamental grasses combined with daisy-type flowers, such as black-eyed Susans and purple cone-flowers, create lovely textures and patterns that are reminiscent of natural ponds. Use large stones as coping and include boulders within the planting design to further enhance the naturalistic feel.

Choose plants for poolside settings with a bit of foresight. Avoid plants that create a constant litter problem, such as maples that drop seedpods, or your pool-cleaning chores will increase. Don't use plants that attract bees, such as beebalm and blue-beard, or you might get stung. And avoid using tall plants except on the north side of the pool or the pool will be shaded and perhaps too cold for an enjoyable swim.

Plants closest to the pool might get splashed by pool water; some plants are sensitive to the chemicals. So choose ones for the edge of the pool that toler-ate a bit of chlorine—these are often salt-tolerant seaside plants such as orna-mental grasses, junipers, and bayberry.

<u>CREATING A SHADY SITTING AREA</u>
You can create shade over a deck or patio by planting a tall tree nearby so that it will cast its cooling shadow dur-ing the hottest part of the day—usually noon and afternoon. Locate the tree about 10 feet to the west of the area that you want shaded. If your deck or patio is large, consider planting the tree in a well in the middle.

If there is no room for a tree, you can easily create shade over a deck or patio with an overhead structure, such as an arbor or trellis. This type of structure provides a wonderful place to grow vines, which can create a leafy bower over your head and deepen the shade. Design the structure from a material and in a style that matches or complements your home's architecture.

The five designs presented in this chap-ter are sure to provide inspiration for creating beautiful plantings close to your outdoor sitting areas. The Fragrant Patio Planting offers a beautiful design filled with plants that perfume the air with various scents from spring through fall. Ornamental Edibles is an innova-tive patio design that looks as beautiful as it tastes. The Naturalistic Pool Planting offers a way to transform a swimming pool into an alluring pond. The Evening Patio Garden features plants that are attractive at night, while the Trellised Deck Planting is a varia-tion on an outdoor room. ❧

Containers of flowering plants bring living color to this deck, which would otherwise look bare and uninviting.

Design: Conni Cross

Relaxing on this patio becomes a delightful sensory experience filled with sweet, flowery fragrances and the music of a bubbling fountain.

Regional Plant Lists

Because climate and growing conditions vary greatly throughout North America, it is impossible to list here specific plants for this landscape plan that would thrive in all regions of the country. However, you can order a Blueprint Package for this plan containing a list of plants, selected by experts, for your region.

The six-page Blueprint Package features a large-size version of this Plan View, plus a detailed Plant and Materials List. It also includes an illustrated list of hundreds of landscape plants suited to your region, to use if you wish to make substitutions, as well as planting instructions and plant adaptation maps to ensure professional-looking results.

See page 157 to order your regionalized Blueprint Package.

FRAGRANT PATIO PLANTING

IMAGINE BEING ENGULFED IN DELICATELY SCENTED AIR as you relax on your patio. You can enjoy such sensory pleasures every day by installing this intricate design filled with fragrant plants. Be sure to provide plenty of seating around the patio so you'll have places to sit and enjoy the perfumed air.

This plan is as adaptable as it is beautiful. The designer includes a patio and combination fountain/planter, but you could plant the border around any existing patio. You might decide to add only a central planter or fountain, or both. You could locate the design right up against your house so that sliding glass or French doors open directly onto the patio—this allows you to enjoy the flowers' perfume from indoors as well. If you choose this option, site the planting so the lattice is directly opposite the wall of the house to capture and hold fragrance.

The central planter and pots scattered about the patio are filled with fragrant annuals and tender perennials. During the cold winter months, try moving the pots to a sunny location inside the house, where they will continue to bloom and perfume the air.

LANDSCAPE PLAN L338 SHOWN IN SUMMER
DESIGNED BY JEFFREY DIEFENBACH

PLAN VIEW

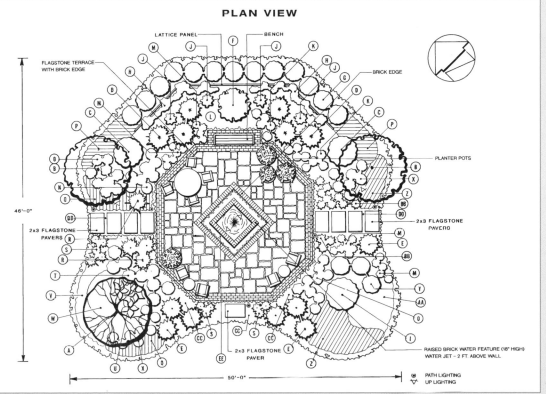

A mouth-watering, colorful and beautiful harvest is always close at hand when you plant this edible design near your front or back door.

Regional Plant Lists

Because climate and growing conditions vary greatly throughout North America, it is impossible to list here specific plants for this landscape plan that would thrive in all regions of the country. However, you can order a Blueprint Package for this plan containing a list of plants, selected by experts, for your region.

The six-page Blueprint Package features a large-size version of this Plan View, plus a detailed Plant and Materials List. It also includes an illustrated list of hundreds of landscape plants suited to your region, to use if you wish to make substitutions, as well as planting instructions and plant adaptation maps to ensure professional-looking results.

See page 157 to order your regionalized Blueprint Package.

ORNAMENTAL EDIBLES

THIS LARGE SEMICIRCULAR BED brimming with beautiful edible plants is designed to be sited either against your house as an extension of your living space, or in any sunny place in your yard for dramatic impact. The garden's plants are chosen for their good looks as well as their edible qualities.

Fruit trees provide shade and a fall harvest, while berry plants double as shrubbery. Smaller herbs, vegetables and fruits fill out the bed, offering food that can be eaten cooked or raw, used as seasoning, or made into tea. There's even one section devoted to a pretty salad garden.

An informal flagstone terrace fills the center of the bed so you can easily putter in the garden or just sit and relax. Flagstone pavers divide the bed into smaller sections and lead into the garden's outer reaches to simplify harvesting and routine maintenance chores, such as weeding. The wooden arbors frame the terrace and create an interesting vertical effect while providing attractive supports for fruiting vines and climbing vegetables.

LANDSCAPE PLAN L339 SHOWN IN SUMMER
DESIGNED BY PATRICK J. DUFFE

PLAN VIEW

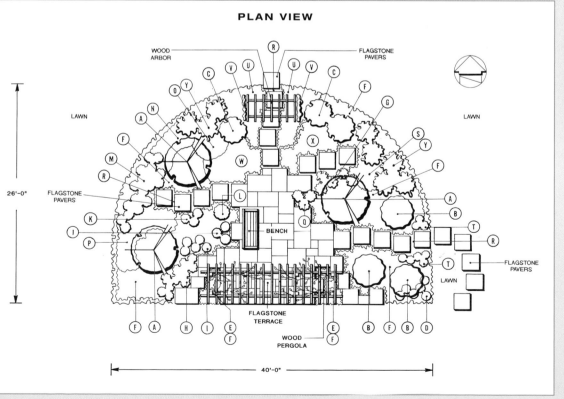

This swimming pool and its naturalistic garden are better than a week's vacation in the country, because they provide months of family enjoyment right in your own backyard. Install the pool and its planting, or adapt the design to beautify an existing swimming pool.

Regional Plant Lists

Because climate and growing conditions vary greatly throughout North America, it is impossible to list here specific plants for this landscape plan that would thrive in all regions of the country. However, you can order a Blueprint Package for this plan containing a list of plants, selected by experts, for your region.

The six-page Blueprint Package features a large-size version of this Plan View, plus a detailed Plant and Materials List. It also includes an illustrated list of hundreds of landscape plants suited to your region, to use if you wish to make substitutions, as well as planting instructions and plant adaptation maps to ensure professional-looking results.

See page 157 to order your regionalized Blueprint Package.

NATURALISTIC POOL PLANTING

HERE'S A NATURAL-LOOKING SWIMMING POOL that the entire family can enjoy. Avid swimmers can plunge into the pool from the dive rock and swim laps, while those more inclined to relaxing can soak in the spa or lounge on the patio. The setting is serene and naturalistic, offering a weekend escape right in your own backyard.

The designer places the front edge of the pool right in the lawn, with an irregular flagstone coping as a natural-looking edge, to create the effect of a real swimming hole. The patio bordering the far side of the pool is elevated two steps on each side to provide the needed height for the waterfall that cascades from the spa into the pool. River rock pavers for the paths, and natural boulders sited strategically in the design, further enhance the pool's natural appearance.

Acting as a privacy screen and windbreak, the background planting consists of various beautifully textured evergreens. An assortment of small shrubs, perennials and ornamental grasses blends into the foreground, creating a soft screen of flowers and foliage that helps integrate the pool into its surroundings.

LANDSCAPE PLAN L340 SHOWN IN SPRING
DESIGNED BY JASON ARGENTIERI

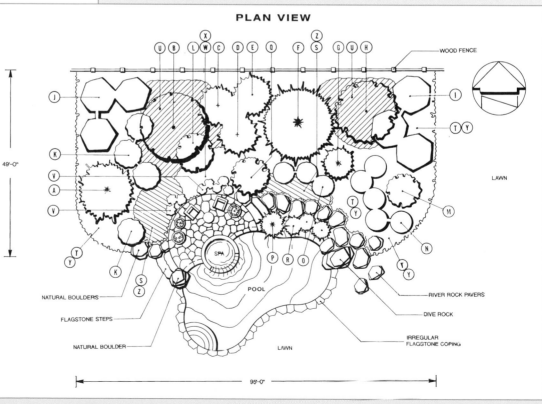

PLAN VIEW

WOOD FENCE

LAWN

NATURAL BOULDERS

FLAGSTONE STEPS

NATURAL BOULDER

SPA

POOL

LAWN

RIVER ROCK PAVERS

DIVE ROCK

IRREGULAR FLAGSTONE COPING

49'-0"

95'-0"

You'll love entertaining outdoors if you install this design, which offers great garden views, musical sound effects and dramatic nighttime lighting.

Regional Plant Lists

Because climate and growing conditions vary greatly throughout North America, it is impossible to list here specific plants for this landscape plan that would thrive in all regions of the country. However, you can order a Blueprint Package for this plan containing a list of plants, selected by experts, for your region.

The six-page Blueprint Package features a large-size version of this Plan View, plus a detailed Plant and Materials List. It also includes an illustrated list of hundreds of landscape plants suited to your region, to use if you wish to make substitutions, as well as planting instructions and plant adaptation maps to ensure professional-looking results.

See page 157 to order your regionalized Blueprint Package.

Evening Patio Garden

THIS PATIO GARDEN IS DESIGNED to be used during summer evenings when people are most likely to sit or entertain guests outdoors. The designer chooses flowers in mostly white and pastel colors that pop out of the shadows and glow in the moonlight. Lamps are strategically placed to provide nighttime lighting; some lamps are used to cast reflections on the formal pool or are directed upward to illuminate the beautifully sculpted tree trunks.

A waterfall cascading as a sheet into the pool creates soothing sound effects. The waterfall flows from a free-standing stone wall that creates a backdrop for the pool. (The mechanism is available as a kit from water garden suppliers.) A stepping-stone island near one edge of the pool allows you to move closer to the waterfall and be immersed in its sound.

This patio garden is designed to be sited in a lawn away from the house, but it can be easily modified to link directly with the house. You can do this by keeping the shape of the patio and extending the plantings and stepping-stones to the house's foundation.

LANDSCAPE PLAN L341 SHOWN IN SUMMER
DESIGNED BY MICHAEL J. OPISSO

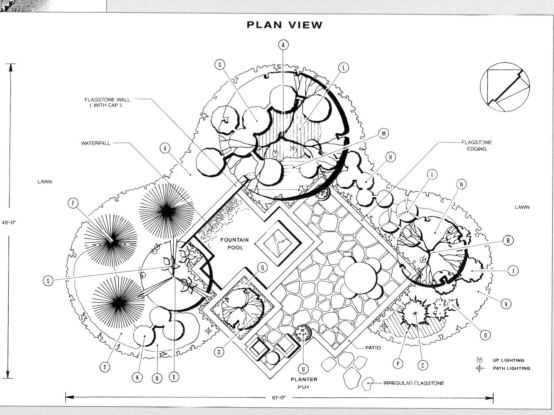

PLAN VIEW

Trellised Deck Planting

A DECK CONNECTED TO A HOUSE truly becomes an outdoor living space when it is linked to the surrounding landscape by a lovely border and a vine-covered overhead structure, as in this design. This border planting contains several small flowering trees, along with low shrubs and an assortment of perennials, to give the deck a feeling of enclosure and intimacy without actually closing it in and blocking views into the rest of the backyard. Vines growing on the overhead trellis create a flowery ceiling and cast pleasant shade on the sitting area.

By widening the border near the deck's stairs and building a wide path of large, irregular paving stones through this part of the garden, the designer visually balances the weight of the deck. The walk and plantings also create a pretty entrance to the deck from the lawn and the rest of the yard, and from the deck to the yard. Two small spring-flowering trees on each side of the walk balance the height of the trellis and soften its vertical lines.

LANDSCAPE PLAN L342 SHOWN IN SUMMER
DESIGNED BY GARY J. MARTIN

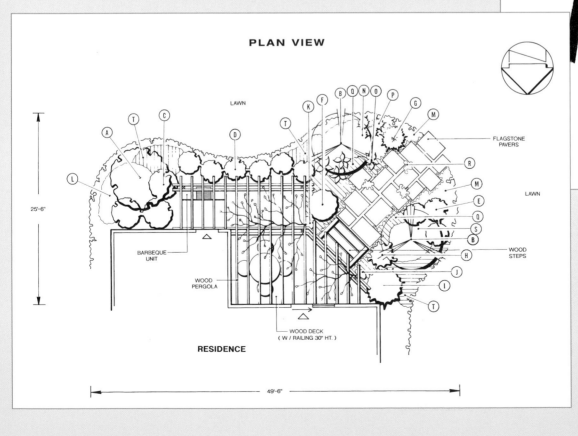

PLAN VIEW

LAWN

FLAGSTONE PAVERS

LAWN

25'-6"

BARBEQUE UNIT

WOOD PERGOLA

WOOD STEPS

WOOD DECK
(W / RAILING 30" HT.)

RESIDENCE

49'-6"

Regional Plant Lists

Because climate and growing conditions vary greatly throughout North America, it is impossible to list here specific plants for this landscape plan that would thrive in all regions of the country. However, you can order a Blueprint Package for this plan containing a list of plants, selected by experts, for your region.

The six-page Blueprint Package features a large-size version of this Plan View, plus a detailed Plant and Materials List. It also includes an illustrated list of hundreds of landscape plants suited to your region, to use if you wish to make substitutions, as well as planting instructions and plant adaptation maps to ensure professional-looking results.

See page 157 to order your regionalized Blueprint Package.

You can extend your living area outdoors and enjoy your deck even more by creating this pretty setting and flower-filled view.

CHAPTER 11

INSTALLING
BEDS AND BORDERS

The plans in this book are designed to help you successfully landscape your property by making the garden areas as beautiful as they can be. There are several ways these professionally designed plans can help make your dream landscape a reality. For instance, if one of the designs in the book suits your yard and your needs, you can use that design exactly as it appears on the pages. Where slight differences between the size of your yard and a plan occur, you can easily adapt a plan—this chapter tells you how. Or you may want to follow a design as a basic recipe, using your own imagination and creativity to customize it to your yard.

To create a long-blooming flower border, plant annuals around the base of spring-flowering bulbs so they'll fill in the gaps left when the bulbs go dormant in early summer.

CHOOSING A PLAN

Study the plans and the renderings in Chapters 3 through 10, concentrating on the ones you think may look attractive on your property. Select the one with the style you like the most, and then proceed with installation, making any necessary adjustments as outlined in this chapter.

Choosing Plants

The plans in this book indicate the layout and placement of plants and hardscape, but they don't specify the exact names of the plants used in the designs. That's because landscape plants are adapted to different climates, and very few are suited to all areas. Even though the plans don't indicate the exact plants to use, you can tell where the designer places different types and sizes of trees, shrubs, groundcovers and perennials by reading the templates (see illustration on page 147). Based on this information, you can then choose your favorite locally adapted plants to carry out the design. Or you can order a complete set of blueprints for any of the plans featured in the book, with a list of plants selected specifically to do well in your region. (See pages 154-158 to order).

After landscape plants are installed and drip irrigation is laid down, the last step is to spread a thick layer or organic mulch over the new bed.

Design: Judy Ogden

Each plan solves the design problem of artistically laying out the bed or border and balancing sizes and shapes. The designer has determined the garden's overall shape and proportions and decided where to best locate a patio, path, hedge or fountain. The basic layout will remain the same, regardless of the particular plants you choose to include. Make sure, however, that the plants are in keeping with the spirit of the bed or border design, as shown in the color illustration, and that they aren't likely to outgrow their allotted space.

ADAPTING A PLAN TO YOUR SITE

Before installing a bed or border design, it's a good idea to create a drawing that accurately depicts the size, shape and important features of your new garden as it will appear in your landscape. There is no other way to know beforehand whether a tree, once mature, will be too close to the house, or a shrub will crowd a walk. The process of making the drawing also tends to generate ideas, and it's certainly quicker to experiment with a pencil and an eraser than with a shovel and your muscles.

Most likely, any bed or border plan in this book will easily fit your property; the designs were created to fit typical properties of various sizes and shapes. If your property varies from these, however, that shouldn't be a major problem, because you can easily adapt the plans to a larger, smaller or differently shaped site. (See page 148.) A good way to start is to site the plan for your new bed or border by placing it on an existing survey of your property. You can do this—even if you aren't an artist—with a few simple tools.

Making a Plan

You'll need tracing paper, pencils, an eraser, a scale ruler and several large sheets of graph paper. Graph paper comes in various sizes, but 18-by-24-inch sheets are the most useful, because they're the same size as the blueprints for the plans in this book.

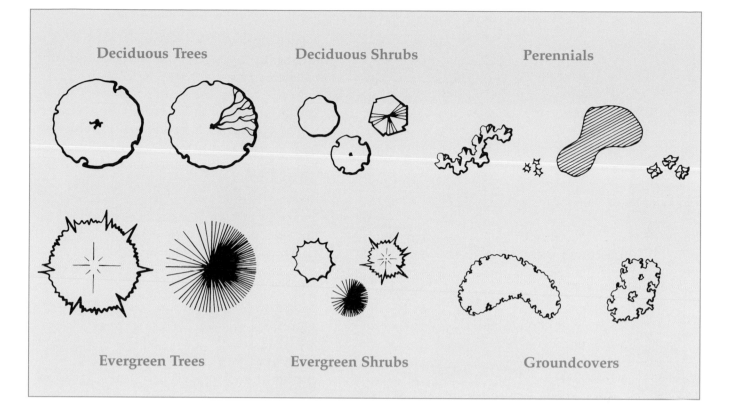

Deciduous Trees • Deciduous Shrubs • Perennials

Evergreen Trees • Evergreen Shrubs • Groundcovers

Although a scale ruler isn't essential, you'll find that it makes measuring to scale much quicker. To make your plan as legible as possible, you may also want to have on hand a T-square, a template of landscape symbols and a compass.

You'll also need an accurate drawing of your existing property. The best way to start is with your property survey. Or you can measure the area where you wish to install the garden yourself. Draw your property's layout using a convenient scale—usually 1 inch of drawing representing either 4 feet (¼ scale) or 8 feet (⅛ scale) of property. (If the scale is too compressed—less than ⅛ scale—details become smaller and more difficult to visualize.) When using a blueprint from one of the plans in this book, you'll find it convenient to use the same scale as the design. Large beds or borders employ ⅛ scale, and those of smaller designs use ¼ scale.

Tracing Your New Design
On tracing paper, accurately redraw the portion of your property where you intend to install the bed or border, enlarging it to fit the chosen scale. (You may wish to draw the layout of your entire property so you can visualize its exact location.) Then add all existing and permanent features that you want to keep, such as pathways, a patio or deck, and walls. Next, add in all existing trees, shrubs and garden areas that you want to keep.

If your house is on the plot plan, note the locations of all doors and windows. This will help you site a garden to take advantage of a view or traffic pattern. Don't guess at the dimensions: use a 50- or 100-foot tape measure and work as precisely as you can. Finally, using a directional arrow, mark which way is north. Once your drawing is complete, photocopy it so you can experiment on the copies and keep the original safe and clean.

Lay the tracing-paper copy of your existing landscape over the blueprint of the bed or border plan from the book, moving it around until you find the best fit. Place another piece of tracing paper on top of the two drawings (use small pieces of tape to keep the sheets aligned), then make adjustments to the layout, if necessary.

The graphic symbols shown here are commonly used on professional landscape designs to indicate different types of plants. Sizes vary to indicate the plants' mature sizes.

You can adapt a landscape plan to a smaller space by judiciously eliminating one or more groups of plants and rearranging other features to create a compact version of the original design. The border design pictured above is the original design; below is a version adapted to a smaller space.

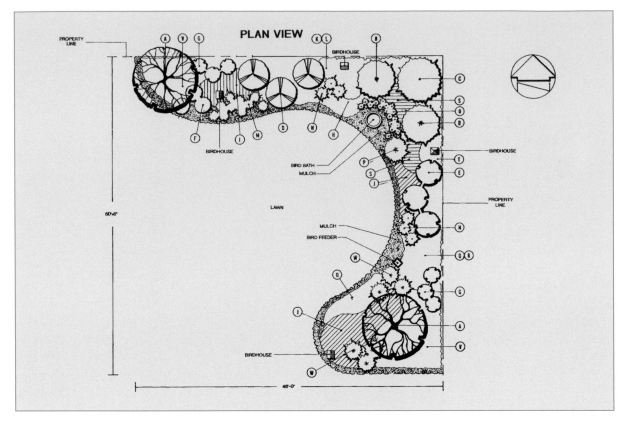

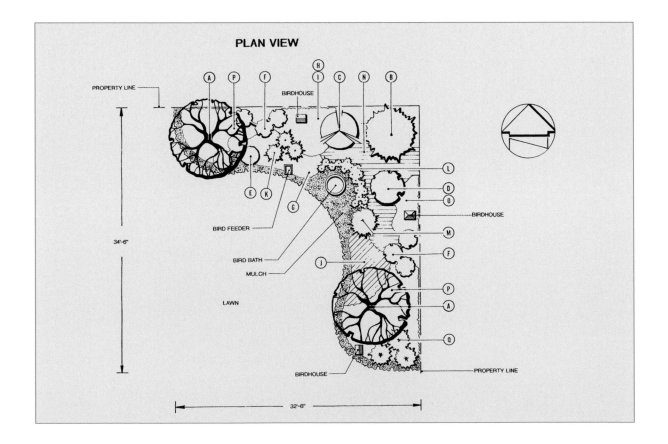

Here's how to do it:

1) Tape a new sheet of tracing paper over both your present plot plan and the bed or border design you wish to adapt.
2) Trace only the permanent features and dimensions of your present yard onto the new sheet of paper.
3) Undo the tape, remove the tracing of the existing plot plan, and shift the new paper over the plan that you wish to adapt, tracing the design's prominent features in slightly different locations.

Adjusting for Lot Size or Shape

Most of the bed and border designs in this book are free-standing or are intended to fit into corners or along the edges of a property, so they are suitable for almost any size lot. However, you may wish to adapt a plan to fill a larger or smaller space on your property, to keep the garden in proportion to its surroundings.

If you expand the perimeter of the original design, don't simply add more space between the designated number of plants. It's important to maintain the right amount of space between individual plants, or the garden will look too sparse or too crowded. Professional designers usually work with odd numbers of plants. You will see one specimen tree or a grouping of three, five or seven shrubs, but rarely a group of two, four or six of a particular plant. When making adjustments, add or subtract plants in a drift or mass planting so that you end up with an odd number.

It's easy to adjust a design to suit a larger site. Simply plant the design according to the plan and increase the number of plants in each group or drift, using the indicated spacing. Adding between three and five plants to a drift is fine, but adding more may change the integrity and scale of the design. If you need to fill a much larger space, try repeating a drift or several drifts of plants from one part of the garden, rather than enlarging a single grouping into a huge mass. Repeating drifts in a garden bed or border creates a pleasing sense of rhythm as your eye travels along and recognizes a pattern.

To adjust a design to a smaller piece of property, take out several plants from each group of plants along the length or width of the design. This reduces the overall scale of the bed or border without destroying the original design.

Adjusting Plans to a Slope

Most of the designs illustrated in Chapters 3 through 10 were created for relatively flat pieces of property or for lots with a slight slope. If your property is more sloped, you can adjust many of these plans to fit, either by regrading or by adding retaining walls. A change of grade involves more than just aesthetics; you may require an engineer or licensed contractor to ensure that changing the grade doesn't create drainage problems. (See below.)

Retaining walls are often used by professional designers to create several flat levels out of steeply sloped ground. The walls are not only functional, but also attractive. You can build walls out of landscape timbers, bricks, stones, or another material that matches your home's architecture. When planning a retaining wall, include drainage pipes at the base to prevent water buildup behind the wall.

Adjusting Grading and Drainage

Even a property that seems flat may not be perfectly flat. Almost every property has some grade (slope) or dips and rises. (The "grade" of a property shouldn't be confused with "grading," which is the term used to describe changing the existing slope.) You should assess the variations in grade on your property and consider any necessary or desired grade changes before finalizing the landscape design.

Grading changes may be minimal or extensive. For example, you may need to flatten a small area for a patio. Or your entire lawn may need grading so that it slopes evenly away from the house toward the street. Some plans call for adding mounds of earth, know as "berms," for effectively screening a view or adding interesting height to an otherwise flat property.

Don't just move soil around the garden or pave large areas without first thinking of the consequences. Before attempting any major changes in grade or before paving large areas near the house, consult a professional to ensure that your plan won't cause drainage problems. He or she can help determine whether some type of drainage tiles or pipes need to be installed, or how to change the grade to avoid any potential problems.

Don't change the grade around the drip line of a large tree, because this can either expose or bury the roots, eventually killing the tree. If it becomes necessary to raise the grade around a tree, construct a well around it to avoid burying the roots.

Solving Drainage Problems

Grading and drainage are interdependent. It's best to grade your property so that water drains away from structures and doesn't collect in beds, borders and paved areas. Proper grading can prevent water from collecting in a basement after heavy rain. It eliminates low areas where water and snow collect instead of draining away properly. Water should drain quickly from paved areas so that the pavement doesn't become an icy hazard or remain unusable for hours after a rainstorm.

Paved areas should maintain a minimum of pitch of ⅛ inch per foot, but ¼ inch is better. A patio that's located next to the house should slope away slightly from the structure. If the patio is located in a lower part of the landscape, where water can't run off because a wall or higher ground surrounds the paving, then you'll need drains and drainage pipes to channel water away. Discuss the matter with a landscape contractor to ensure a practical and economical solution. You may also need to consult utility companies to determine the location of any underground pipes and cables.

Installing the Garden Design

Whether you plant a garden and construct walkways, a deck or a patio yourself, or hire a contractor to do all or part of the work, check local building codes before you begin any extensive landscaping. Many communities have building codes that may affect the height of shrubs, walls and fences at the property line, especially along the street. Permanent structures and home improvements, such as decks, patios and retaining walls, may require a building permit.

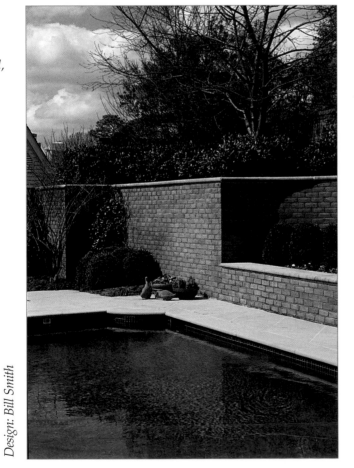

A brick wall can be both ornamental and practical, creating a private and safe place to swim.

Design: Bill Smith

Communities often require proof of proper engineering and, in most cases, demand that such structures be a certain distance from the property line. While swimming pools almost always require a fence or enclosure to prevent small children from accidentally wandering into the area, a garden pool may also need a fence if it is more than 18 inches deep. It's your responsibility to find out which regulations in your community, if any, apply to landscaping.

Getting Ready to Plant

Before planting, it's important to prepare the soil thoroughly so that the plants stay healthy. The best way to start is with a soil test. Contact your local County Extension Service or a private soil-testing laboratory. Along with the results, you'll get detailed recommendations on how to improve the soil. These will most likely include adding organic matter, such as composted bark or sawdust. Spread 2 or 3 inches of the organic material over the soil where you'll be planting, and till it in. Additional fertilizer, and perhaps lime or sulfur to adjust the soil pH, may also be recommended.

Removing Lawn

There are several ways to remove an existing lawn where new beds and borders, walkways, or a patio will go. You can strip the lawn away just below the roots with a spade, or you can rent a power sod cutter. (Sod that's stripped off can be saved and transplanted where it's needed. If you have no need for the sod, use it as fill or add it to the compost pile.) Lawns can also be killed with an herbicide such a glyphosate, but be careful not to spray the chemical accidentally on desirable plants, or you'll kill them. Or, if you prefer, you can smother an existing lawn under a deep layer of mulch.

Marking the Garden Plan

Once you've cleared the area to be landscaped, use a measuring tape to mark the outlines of the new garden. You can use wood or metal stakes and run strings between them to show clearly where everything will be located. A garden hose or a clothesline works well to outline beds and borders. A sprinkling of garden lime or flour also works well to trace outlines and mark planting locations. You'll want to place markers to indicate areas of major construction, such as a deck, pool or walkway, and to mark the sites of major trees.

When you are ready to plant, set out out all the plants intended for the garden according to the planting plan, but don't remove them from their containers. Study their locations from several angles and make adjustments as needed before you plant. Then mark their holes with lime or flour and dig the holes. Remove each plant from its container one at a time, just before planting, to prevent the roots from drying out. (See page 152 for planting instructions.)

PLANT SHOPPING

The plants specified on the blueprint you order should be available at a high-quality local nursery or through mail-order catalogs. If you're buying from a catalog, it's best to find a company that's located in the same—or nearly the same—zone as your own. For example, if you live in northern California, try to buy plants from a catalog whose nursery is located on the West

Mark the placement of a new bed before you strip off the lawn, by sprinkling garden lime along the outlines.

Coast. The best selection is often available in spring, but fall is a wonderful time to plant, too. Summer planting is more stressful on plants, but container-grown plants respond well to summer planting if they are kept watered during periods of heat and drought.

Choosing and Planting Trees and Shrubs
Trees and shrubs are available as dormant bare-root, balled-and-burlapped (B&B) or container-grown plants. Both bare-root and B&B plants are grown in native soil in nursery fields. Bare-roots are dug while they're dormant, and the soil is washed off. Since they're quite perishable, they should be planted promptly. B&B plants can survive for weeks before planting, but it's wise to keep them shaded and moist. Bare-root plants are best planted in late winter, and B&B plants in early spring or fall, soon after they're dug up.

Container-grown trees and shrubs are increasingly more common and can be installed anytime without suffering transplant shock, since their root systems are completely intact. Before removing a plant from its container, check to see if the soil is moist. If not, water the plant thoroughly and allow the soil to drain. When it's moist—not dry or soggy—it's much easier to handle and less prone to fall apart. Hold the plant upside down or lay it sideways on the ground, and let it fall or slide gently out of the container. When planting a container-grown tree or shrub, always be sure to loosen and untangle any matted or circling roots. A tree or shrub whose roots circle the trunk will eventually die.

Set the plant in the hole and check the height of the rootball. To allow the soil to settle, the top of the rootball should be slightly higher than the surrounding garden soil. When you are satisfied with the planting height, backfill the hole halfway, add water, then finish backfilling enough to slightly cover the top of the rootball.

To help the soil retain water and direct it to the roots, make a ring of raised soil around the plant and flood the basin several times with water. After planting, apply an organic mulch, such as wood chips, over the soil to keep it moist and weed-free. Also be sure to check that any ties used to stake a tree are not cutting into the bark. Do not leave a tree staked any longer than a year. Then be sure to remove all stakes, wires and ties; if left in place, they can girdle the tree and do serious damage.

Choosing and Planting Groundcovers
Many groundcovers are sold in flats or packs. Space them uniformly—usually five pachysandra, three English ivy or three periwinkle plants for every square foot. For quicker coverage, plant closer together; to save money, plant farther apart, although the plants will take longer to fill in. Apply mulch to keep the planting weed-free until the groundcover fills in.

Choosing and Planting Perennials, Annuals and Bulbs
Nurseries usually sell perennials in quart, 1-gallon or 2-gallon containers at the height of their bloom time. Mail-order companies normally ship very young plants in small pots, or more mature

To correctly plant a tree or shrub, dig a hole no deeper than the rootball but twice as wide. Leave real burlap on the rootball because it rots, but remove plastic burlap, which doesn't rot. Refill the hole with native soil and build a berm to hold water. Stake a tree loosely, and be sure to remove ties and stakes after one year.

plants as bare-root specimens. Whether you buy small, young plants or larger, more mature plants, remember that they will spread considerably—both upward and outward—as they grow. If you're uncertain about a plant's mature height and spread, ask the nursery staff or check the tag before you plant.

Buy annuals from your local garden center, start them from seed indoors, or sow seeds directly in the garden after the last frost in your area. Garden centers usually sell annuals in divided plastic containers called "cell packs," or in small pots.

Whether you're choosing perennials or annuals, look for healthy plants with dark green foliage, free of insect or other damage. Lift the pot up and check underneath; if you see a tangle of roots poking through the drainage holes, don't buy the plant—a rootbound plant is less likely to survive the stress of transplanting.

You can buy wonderful bulbs from mail-order catalogs or at local garden centers. If you go out and select bulbs yourself, make sure you mark each bag so you'll know what you've got when you get home. Bulbs are sold when they are normally planted—in either spring or fall.

Bulbs are usually most effective when planted in large drifts. There's no need to dig 50 individual holes, though. Just dig a single large hole to the proper depth and scatter the bulbs at varying distances from each other along the bottom of the hole. That way, you'll get the same naturalistic effect with less effort. Many of the plans in this book show bulbs and perennials growing together in the same space. Bulbs can be added to drifts of perennials at fall

planting time by digging holes among the young perennial plants, taking care to avoid their crowns and main roots, and placing several bulbs in each hole.

HIRING A LANDSCAPE CONTRACTOR

The virtue of the plans offered in this book is that you can enjoy the benefits of a professional design without paying what you would for custom work. Handy do-it-

An important, but often overlooked, step in planting a container-grown perennial or shrub is to loosen the roots. This encourages the roots to grow outward and establish a strong foothold in the surrounding soil.

yourselfers can easily manage the variety of tasks required to install a bed or border. Others may wish to hire a landscape contractor to do some or all of the installation.

Ask your friends and neighbors for recommendations for a contractor, but be sure to see examples of their work and check their references before you hire anyone. Once you've decided on an individual, write out a contract that specifies work and payment schedules.

When your bed or border is finished, the property will have a beautiful look that you and your family will enjoy for years to come. The new garden will improve your outdoor living environment the day it's completed, and the initial investment will more than pay for itself over the years by adding to the value of your home. ❁

THE LANDSCAPE BLUEPRINT PACKAGE

THE LANDSCAPE BLUEPRINT PACKAGE
AVAILABLE FROM HOME PLANNERS

includes all the necessary information you need to lay out and install the landscape design of your choice. Professionally designed and prepared with attention to detail, these clear, easy-to-follow plans offer everything from a precise plot plan and regionalized plant and materials list to helpful sheets on installing your landscape and determining the mature size of your plants. These plans will help you achieve professional-looking results, adding value and enjoyment to your property for years to come.

Each set of blueprints is a full 18"x 24" in size with clear, complete instructions and easy-to-read type. Consisting of six detailed sheets, these plans show how all plants and materials are put together to form an exciting landscape for your home.

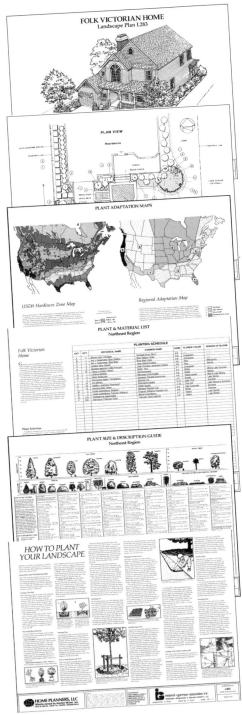

FRONTAL SHEET
This artist's line sketch shows a typical house (if applicable) and all the elements of the finished landscape when plants are at or near maturity. This will give you a visual image or "picture" of the design and what you might expect your property to look like when fully landscaped.

PLAN VIEW
This is an aerial view of the property showing the exact placement of all landscape elements, including symbols and call-outs for flowers, shrubs, groundcovers, walkways, walls, gates and other garden amenities. This sheet is the key to the design and shows you the contour, spacing, flow and balance of all the elements in the design, as well as providing an exact "map" for laying out your property.

ZONE MAPS
These two informative maps offer detailed information to help you better select and judge the performance of your plants. Map One is a United States Department of Agriculture Hardiness Zone Map that shows the average low temperatures by zones in various parts of the United States and Canada. The "Zone" listing for plants on Sheet 3 of your Plant and Materials List is keyed to this map. Map Two is a Regional Adaptation Map, which takes into account other factors beyond low temperatures, such as rainfall, humidity, extremes of temperature, and soil acidity or alkalinity. Both maps are key to plant adaptability and are used for the selection of landscape plants for your plans.

REGIONALIZED PLANT & MATERIALS LIST
Keyed to the Plan View sheet, this page lists all of the plants and materials necessary to execute the design. It gives the quantity, botanical name, common name, flower color, season of bloom and hardiness zones for each plant specified. This becomes your "shopping list" for dealing with contractors or buying the plants and materials yourself. Most importantly, the plants shown on this page have been chosen by a team of professional horticulturalists for their adaptability, availability and performance in your specific part of the country.

PLANT SIZE & DESCRIPTION GUIDE
Because you may have trouble visualizing certain plants, this handy regionalized guide provides a scale and silhouettes to help you determine the final height and shape of various trees and shrubs in your landscape plan. It also provides a quick means of choosing alternate plants appropriate to your region in case you do not wish to install a certain tree or shrub, or if you cannot find the plant at local nurseries.

PLANTING & MAINTAINING YOUR LANDSCAPE
This valuable sheet gives handy information and illustrations on purchasing plant materials, preparing your site and caring for your landscape after installation. Includes quick, helpful advice on planting trees, shrubs and groundcovers, staking trees, establishing a lawn, watering, weed control and pruning.

LANDSCAPE REGIONS

TO ORDER YOUR PLANS,

simply find the Plan Number of the design of your choice in the Plans Index below. Consult the Price Schedule to determine the price of your plans, choosing the 1-set package for Landscape Plans and any additional or reverse sets you desire. If ordering Landscape Plans, make sure your Plant and Materials List contains the best selection for your area by referring to the Regional Order Map below and specifying the region in which you will be building. Fill out the Order Coupon and mail it to us for prompt fulfillment or call our Toll-Free Order Hotline for even faster service.

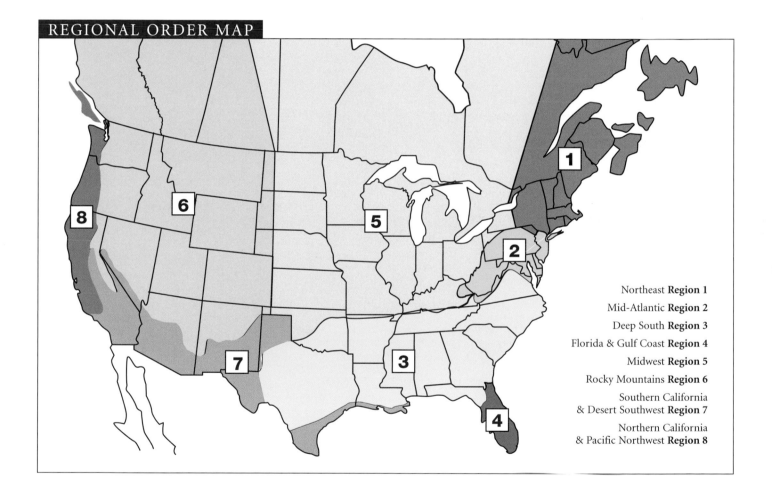

REGIONAL ORDER MAP

Northeast **Region 1**
Mid-Atlantic **Region 2**
Deep South **Region 3**
Florida & Gulf Coast **Region 4**
Midwest **Region 5**
Rocky Mountains **Region 6**
Southern California
& Desert Southwest **Region 7**
Northern California
& Pacific Northwest **Region 8**

TO USE THE INDEX, refer to the design number listed in numerical order (a helpful page reference is also given). Note the price tier and refer to the Blueprint Price Schedule for the cost of one, four or eight sets of blueprints or the cost of a reproducible drawing. Additional prices are shown for identical and reverse blueprint sets.

TO ORDER, Call toll free 1-800-521-6797 for current pricing and availability prior to mailing the order form.
FAX: 1-800-224-6699 or 520-544-3086.

BLUEPRINT PRICE SCHEDULE

Prices guaranteed through December 31, 2002

TIERS	1-SET STUDY PACKAGE	4-SET BUILDING PACKAGE	8-SET BUILDING PACKAGE	1-SET REPRODUCIBLE*
P2	$40	$70	$110	$160
P3	$70	$100	$140	$190
P4	$100	$130	$170	$220

* Requires a fax number

OPTIONS FOR PLANS IN TIERS P2–P4

Additional Identical Blueprints in same order for "P2–P4" price plans ....**$10 per set**
Reverse Blueprints (mirror image) for "P2–P4" price plans ....**$10 fee per order**

PLAN INDEX

ORDER FORM

DISCLAIMER

The designers we work with have put substantial care and effort into the creation of their blueprints. However, because they cannot provide on-site consultation, supervision and control over actual construction, and because of the great variance in local building requirements, building practices and soil, seismic, weather and other conditions, WE CANNOT MAKE ANY WARRANTY, EXPRESS OR IMPLIED, WITH RESPECT TO THE CONTENT OR USE OF THE BLUE-PRINTS, INCLUDING BUT NOT LIMITED TO ANY WARRANTY OF MERCHANTABILITY OR OF FITNESS FOR A PARTICULAR PURPOSE. **ITEMS, PRICES, TERMS AND CONDITIONS ARE SUBJECT TO CHANGE WITHOUT NOTICE. REPRODUCIBLE PLAN ORDERS MAY REQUIRE A CUSTOMER'S SIGNED RELEASE BEFORE SHIPPING.**

TERMS AND CONDITIONS

These designs are protected under the terms of United States Copyright Law and may not be copied or reproduced in any way, by any means, unless you have purchased Reproducibles which clearly indicate your right to copy or reproduce. We authorize the use of your chosen design as an aid in the construction of one single family home only. You may not use this design to build a second or multiple dwellings without purchasing another blueprint or blueprints or paying additional design fees.

HOW MANY BLUEPRINTS DO YOU NEED?

Although a standard building package may satisfy many states, cities and counties, some plans may require certain changes. For your convenience, we have developed a Reproducible plan which allows a local professional to modify and make up to 10 copies of your revised plan. As our plans are all copyright protected, with your purchase of the Reproducible, we will supply you with a Copyright release letter. The number of copies you may need: 1 for owner; 3 for builder; 2 for local building department and 1-3 sets for your mortgage lender.

ORDER TOLL FREE!
FOR INFORMATION ABOUT ANY OF OUR SERVICES OR TO ORDER CALL

1-800-521-6797
Browse our website:
www.eplans.com

BLUEPRINTS ARE NOT REFUNDABLE EXCHANGES ONLY

FOR CUSTOMER SERVICE,
CALL TOLL FREE **1-888-690-1116.**

HOME PLANNERS, LLC
Wholly owned by Hanley-Wood, LLC
3275 WEST INA ROAD, SUITE 110
TUCSON, ARIZONA 85741

THE BASIC BLUEPRINT PACKAGE

Rush me the following (please refer to the Plans Index and Price Schedule in this section):

_____ Set(s) of reproducibles*, plan number(s) _____ $_____

_____ Set(s) of blueprints, plan number(s) _____ $_____

_____ Additional identical blueprints (standard or reverse) in same order @ $50 per set $_____

POSTAGE AND HANDLING (signature is required for all deliveries)		
CARRIER DELIVERY		
No CODs (Requires street address—No P.O.Boxes)		
• **Regular Service** (Allow 7–10 business days for delivery)	$8.00	$_____
• **Priority** (Allow 4–5 business days for delivery)	$12.00	$_____
• **Express** (Allow 3 business days for delivery)	$22.00	$_____
Overseas Delivery	Phone, FAX or Mail for Quote	

NOTE: All delivery times are from date blueprint package is shipped.

POSTAGE (from box above) $_____

SUBTOTAL $_____

SALES TAX (AZ & MI residents, please add appropriate state & local sales tax.) $_____

TOTAL (Subtotal and Tax) $_____

YOUR ADDRESS (please print legibly)

Name _____

Street _____

City _____ State _____ ZIP _____

Daytime telephone number (required) _____

* Fax number (required for reproducible orders) _____

TeleCheck® Checks By Phone℠ available

FOR CREDIT CARD ORDERS ONLY Please fill in the information below:

Credit card number_____ Exp: Month/Year _____

Check One: ❑ Visa ❑ MasterCard ❑ Discover Card ❑ American Express

Signature (required) _____

Please check appropriate box: ❑ Licensed Builder-Contractor ❑ Homeowner

ORDER TOLL FREE 1-800-521-6797
BY FAX: Copy the order form above and send it on our FAXLINE:
1-800-224-6699 or 520-544-3086

Order Form Key
HPT514

BEFORE FILLING OUT THE ORDER FORM, PLEASE CALL US ON OUR TOLL-FREE BLUEPRINT HOTLINE 1-800-521-6797. YOU MAY WANT TO LEARN MORE ABOUT OUR SERVICES AND PRODUCTS. HERE'S SOME INFORMATION YOU WILL FIND HELPFUL.

OUR EXCHANGE POLICY

With the exception of reproducible plan orders, we will exchange your entire first order for an equal or greater number of blueprints within our plan collection within 90 days of the original order. The entire content of your original order must be returned before an exchange will be processed. Please call our customer service department for your return authorization number and shipping instructions. If the returned blueprints look used, redlined or copied, we will not honor your exchange. Fees for exchanging your blueprints are as follows: 20% of the amount of the original order...plus the difference in cost if exchanging for a design in a higher price bracket or less the difference in cost if exchanging for a design in a lower price bracket. **(Reproducible blueprints are not exchangeable or refundable.)** Please call for current postage and handling prices. Shipping and handling charges are not refundable. Please call our customer service department for your return authorization number and shipping instructions.

ABOUT REPRODUCIBLES

When purchasing a reproducible you may be required to furnish a fax number. The designer will fax documents that you must sign and return to them before shipping will take place.

ABOUT REVERSE BLUEPRINTS

Although lettering and dimensions will appear backward, reverses will be a useful aid if you decide to flop the plan. See Price Schedule and Plans Index for pricing.

REVISING, MODIFYING AND CUSTOMIZING PLANS

Like many homeowners who buy these plans, you and your builder, architect or engineer may want to make changes to them. We recommend purchase of a reproducible plan for any changes made by your builder, licensed architect or engineer. As set forth below, we cannot assume any responsibility for blueprints which have been changed, whether by you, your builder or by professionals selected by you or referred to you by us, because such individuals are outside our supervision and control.

ARCHITECTURAL AND ENGINEERING SEALS

Some cities and states are now requiring that a licensed architect or engineer review and "seal" a blueprint, or officially approve it, prior to construction due to concerns over energy costs, safety and other factors. Prior to application for a building permit or the start of actual construction, we strongly advise that you consult your local building official who can tell you if such a review is required.

ABOUT THE DESIGNS

The architects and designers whose work appears in this publication are among America's leading residential designers. Each plan was designed to meet the requirements of a nationally recognized model building code in effect at the time and place the plan was drawn. Because national building codes change from time to time, plans may not comply with any such code at the time they are sold to a customer. In addition, building officials may not accept these plans as final construction documents of record as the plans may need to be modified and additional drawings and details added to suit local conditions and requirements. We strongly advise that purchasers consult a licensed architect or engineer, and their local building official, before starting any construction related to these plans.

LOCAL BUILDING CODES AND ZONING REQUIREMENTS

At the time of creation, our plans are drawn to specifications published by the Building Officials and Code Administrators (BOCA) International, Inc.; the Southern Building Code Congress (SBCCI) International, Inc.; the International Conference of Building Officials (ICBO); or the Council of American Building Officials (CABO). Our plans are designed to meet or exceed national building standards. Because of the great differences in geography and climate throughout the United States and Canada, each state, county and municipality has its own building codes, zone requirements, ordinances and building regulations. Your plan may need to be modified to comply with local requirements regarding snow loads, energy codes, soil and seismic conditions and a wide range of other matters. In addition, you may need to obtain permits or inspections from local governments before and in the course of construction. Prior to using blueprints ordered from us, we strongly advise that you consult a licensed architect or engineer—and speak with your local building official—before applying for any permit or beginning construction. We authorize the use of our blueprints on the express condition that you strictly comply with all local building codes, zoning requirements and other applicable laws, regulations, ordinances and requirements. Notice: Plans for homes to be built in Nevada must be re-drawn by a Nevada-registered professional. Consult your building official for more information on this subject.

**TOLL FREE
1-800-521-6797**

REGULAR OFFICE HOURS:
8:00 a.m.-9:00 p.m. EST, Monday-Friday

If we receive your order by 3:00 p.m. EST, Monday-Friday, we'll process it and ship within **two business days**. When ordering please have your credit card or check information ready. We'll also ask you for the Order Form Key Number at the bottom of the order form.
By FAX: Copy the Order Form on the next page and send it on our FAX line: 1-800-224-6699 or 520-544-3086.

Canadian Customers
Order Toll Free 1-877-223-6389

INDEX